ABRACADABRA
TO
ZOMBIE

ABRACADABRA TO ZOMBIE

Don & Pam Wulffson

illustrations by Jared Lee

MORE THAN 300 WACKY WORD ORIGINS

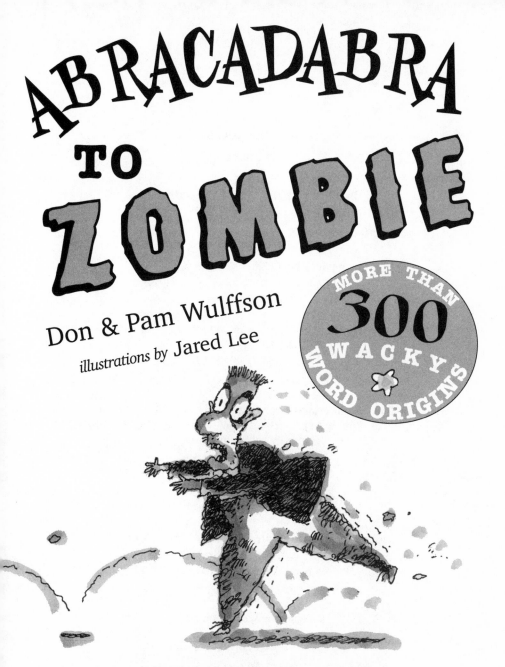

DUTTON CHILDREN'S BOOKS

New York

For Jennifer and Gwen

D. W. & P. W.

For Les and Carolyn Jerdon

J. L.

Library of Congress Cataloging-in-Publication Data
Wulffson, Don L.
Abracadabra to zombie: more than 300 wacky word origins/
Don and Pam Wulffson; illustrated by Jared Lee.—1st ed.
p. cm.
Summary: Provides the stories behind the meanings of such common words
and phrases as Adidas, Jeep, ketchup, peeping Tom, tuxedo, and Yankees.
ISBN 0-525-47100-6
1. English language—Etymology—Dictionaries, Juvenile. [1. English language—
Etymology.] I. Wulffson, Pam. II. Lee, Jared D., ill. III. Title.
PE1580.W85 2003
422'.03—dc21   2003040812

Published in the United States by Dutton Children's Books,
a division of Penguin Young Readers Group
345 Hudson Street, New York, New York 10014
www.penguin.com

Designed by Richard Amari

Printed in USA
First Edition
3 5 7 9 10 8 6 4 2

Words have ancestors, too.
It's great fun to trace them.

FROM *The Romance of Words,* BY DR. ERNEST WEEKLEY

Introduction

*L*ollipops. How come they're called that?

Or *Smokey the Bear*. Was he a real bear or just a made-up one?

And *Pearl Jam*. How did the group come up with a name as weird as that?

From the clothes you wear to the things you eat, from the sports you play to the movies you see—behind the name of everything in your life, there's a story. Most of the stories are just fun and informative—like how one of the NFL's football teams is named after a poem. Others are really surprising. Take *limousines,* for example. They used to be things people walked around with on their heads!

Most of the words in this book—from *abracadabra* to *zombie*—are ones you know. You won't be surprised by the words, just by how they came to be. The only exception is the group at the end. They're "Forgotten Words," whose meanings have been lost over time. Like a *quakebuttocks*. You've probably seen a few of them, and even knew what they were. You just called them by a different name—cowards!

The history of a word is called "etymology"; a brief etymology is given for every word in the dictionary, either before or after its definition. Take the word *diaper,* for example:

> di·a·per (dī′pər, dī′ə pər) *n.* [ME. < OF. *diapre, diaspre.* kind of ornamented cloth < ML. *diasprum.* flowered cloth. altered (after *dia-,* DIA-, because of ML. pronun. of initial *j*-) < *jaspis* < L. *iaspis,* JASPER] 1. *a)* orig., cloth or fabric with a pattern of repeated small figures, such as diamonds *b)* a napkin, towel, etc. of such cloth *c)* such a pattern, as in art 2. a soft, absorbent cloth folded and arranged between the legs and around the waist of a baby —*vt.* 1. to give a diaper design to 2. to put a fresh diaper on (a baby)*

*From *Webster's New World Dictionary,* 2nd College Edition/Revised School Printing, edited by David B. Guralnik (New York: Simon & Schuster, 1985).

The etymology section at the beginning of this dictionary entry tells you what the word meant in each of the languages through which it passed, with its most ancient form and meaning given last. Among other things, it indicates that the word first appeared in Latin (L.) and meant "jasper," a type of precious green stone. Next, in Medieval Latin (ML.) it referred to "flowered cloth." Finally, it tells you that in Old French (OF.) it came to mean "ornamented cloth," and this word and meaning were absorbed into Middle English (ME.).

Sometimes people disagree about a word's history. Take *palomino*, for example. One story has it that Hernán Cortés, the Spanish conqueror of Mexico, gave one of these golden tan, white-maned horses to his friend Juan Palomino, by which name they've been known ever since. The other story is that the horse takes its name from *paloma*, Spanish for "a dovelike bird" with similar markings.

Which story is the correct one? To be honest, it's impossible to tell. Both stories make sense; both appear reasonable. We don't mean to be quakebuttocks about it, but we've tried to avoid such words. Only when we were sure we had strong enough evidence to back up one meaning rather than another did the story get included. And it had to measure up to another of our strict standards: it had to be a story that would amuse and maybe even *gloppen* you!

ABRACADABRA

TO

ZOMBIE

ABRACADABRA ■ The word *abracadabra* is all part of the fun and games of modern magic acts. But in the beginning, centuries ago, the word was taken very seriously. *Abracadabra* was a one-word spell used to protect people against disease. There are many stories about its origin. Some think that the word derives from the Hebrew phrase *abreq ad Habra,* meaning "hurl your thunderbolt even unto death."

A physician of the 14th century gave precise instructions as to the use of the mystical word: The paper on which abracadabra was written had to be folded in the form of a cross and suspended from the neck by a strip of linen in such a way that the paper rested on the abdomen for nine days. Before the sunrise of the tenth day, the person was instructed to cast the amulet over his or her shoulder into a stream running to the east.

During the horror of the Black Death (bubonic plague) in Europe throughout the 14th century, people wore amulets—"magic charms"—believing this would protect them against the disease. Hanging by a strip of linen around the neck, the amulet was in the shape of an upside-down triangle.

ABRACADABRA
ABRACADABR
ABRACADAB
ABRACADA
ABRACAD
ABRACA
ABRAC
ABRA
ABR
AB
A

Each line of the triangle lost a letter in the word until only *A* remained. As the letters disappeared, so supposedly did the illness. Later generations adopted the first line of the triangle to stand for the whole. In time, the amulets were tossed, but the first line—the word *abracadabra*—continued to be chanted in the belief that it offered protection from the plague and other illnesses.

> The Black Death got its name from the fact that it causes hemorrhaging under the skin, which shows up as black spots and blotches. The disease killed millions—as much as two-thirds of the population of many countries in Asia and Europe.

ADIDAS® ■ In 1920, at the age of twenty, Adolph (Adi) Dassler of Germany, the son of a cobbler, invented spiked shoes for track and field. Later, Adi made shoes for all sorts of sports, such as boxing, baseball, and golf.

> Muhammad Ali and Joe Frazier were both wearing Adidas boxing shoes in their "Fight of the Century" in 1971.

The name *Adidas* is an acronym (a word made from letters of other words). In this case, it's from the name of the inventor, Adi Dassler.

(See Nike®, page 79, and Tennis Shoes, page 124.)

AFRICA ■ *Afar*, Arabic for "desert," is the name of a barren region in northeastern Africa. When the Romans conquered *Afar* in 264 B.C., they took the name to mean the continent's entire landmass. In English, *Afar* evolved into *Africa*.

AIR FORCE ONE ■ Presidential air transport began in 1944 with Franklin Roosevelt. But at the time, the plane wasn't called *Air Force One*. Roosevelt jokingly named it the *Sacred Cow*, a term for something regarded as holy and untouchable. From 1947 to 1953, President Harry Truman flew in the *Independence*, which he named after his home-

town—Independence, Missouri. From 1954 to 1961, President Dwight D. Eisenhower traveled aboard a VC-121E. His wife, Mamie, christened it the *Columbine III* in honor of the state flower of her adopted state, Colorado.

One day in 1953, two aircraft with the call sign 8610 were in the air at the same time—one of which carried the President of the United States. Realizing that the presidential plane needed a special call sign, "Air Force One" was

> *Among other nicknames, Air Force One is called "The Flying White House" or "The Flying Oval Office."*

adopted. For the next eight years, the term was top secret; it not only identified the plane but also when the president was aboard and in the air. This was changed by John F. Kennedy in 1961: he declassified it and used it exclusively as the name of the craft.

ALIBI ■ An *alibi* is an excuse or explanation of why a person did not have the opportunity to commit a crime. The term is a Latin word meaning "elsewhere."

ALICE'S ADVENTURES IN WONDERLAND ■ One day in England in 1862, a mathematics teacher took three little girls on a picnic. The man was Charles Lutwidge Dodgson. The girls were sisters—Alice, Lorina, and Edith Liddell. During the outing, Dodgson made up a fanciful tale about a girl who fell down a rabbit hole into a strange land. Ten-year-old Alice was

> *Carroll coined (invented) many new words and used them in his books. Several—such as squawk, mad hatter, and tweedledee—have become enjoyable additions to the English language.*

Dodgson's favorite. To please her, he used her name for the heroine of the story.

Alice loved the story and begged Dodgson to write it down. That night, at one sitting, he wrote *Alice's Adventures Underground.* Later, Dodgson expanded the story and changed its title to *Alice's Adventures in Wonderland.* The book was published in 1865, and its sequel, *Through the Looking-Glass,* followed in 1872.

> *Dodgson wrote under a pen name, Lewis Carroll, which he devised by translating his first and middle names (Charles Lutwidge) into Latin, reversing them, and then translating them back into English.*

ALLEN, WOODY ■ Growing up in Brooklyn, he was Allen Stewart Konigsberg. Said the deadpan comedian: "I told the other kids my name was Frank, but they still beat me up."

OTHER MOVIE STARS' REAL NAMES
Bruce Lee = Lee Yuen Kam
Cher = Cherilyn Sarkisian
Chuck Norris = Carlos Ray
John Wayne = Marion Morrison
Marilyn Monroe = Norma Jean Mortenson (later Baker)
Nicholas Cage = Nicholas Coppola
Raquel Welch = Raquel Tejada
Susan Sarandon = Susan Tomaling
Tom Cruise = Thomas Mapother IV
Whoopi Goldberg = Caryn Johnson

ALPHABET ■ Not only did the idea for our modern alphabet come from the Greeks, but the word *alphabet* itself was made by joining the first two Greek letters—*alpha* and *beta*.

The English alphabet has gone through many changes since people began using it. For one thing, it has gotten longer. Believe it or not, our alphabet once had only twenty-two letters. The missing letters were *j, k, u,* and *w.*

During the Middle Ages, the letter *j* was created out of the letter *i.* This is the reason why *j* follows *i* in the alphabet and why these are the only two letters that are dotted.

About the same time, the letter *k* was created as a substitute for the letter *c.* The reason for making this new letter was that *c* did not have a "hard" enough sound for certain words. For example, until *k* was invented, the word king had to be spelled *cyng.*

You have probably noticed that *u* and *v* look much alike. The reason for this is that *u* was once a form of the letter *v.* Not until the 18th century was it established as a vowel symbol only.

Perhaps the most interesting of the letters is that which follows *u* and *v*—*w.* At one time, this letter was written as a double *v* (*vv*) or a double *u* (*uu*). Over the years, the "double *u*" become the letter *w.*

AMAZON RIVER ■ Greek mythology describes a race of giant women warriors called the Amazons. In 1541, while descending the largest river in South America, Spanish explorer Francisco de Orellana battled tribes of big, tough female warriors. He dubbed them Amazons because they reminded him of the mythic warriors of the Greeks. He called the river the Amazon, due to its incredible size and power.

Although it now empties into the Atlantic Ocean, the Amazon once flowed into the Pacific! (About 65 million years ago, the uplift of the Andes Mountains made the Amazon flow in a new—eastward—direction.)

AMERICA ■ Amerigo Vespucci, after whom America was named, was a banker and part-time mapmaker. After he lost his banking job, he went to sea with Columbus as a mapmaker. Seeing Amerigo's maps of the new continent, people began calling it America.

Though native peoples had been living on the continent for thousands of years, it is widely believed that the Vikings and the Chinese (among others) reached America long before Columbus. The Vikings, landing on the east coast, called the place Vinland (Wineland); the Chinese, reaching the west coast (Mexico, especially), called the place Fusang, which is the Chinese name for a type of tree growing in the area.

ARGENTINA ■ Pioneers in this South American country discovered a great deal of silver. When it declared independence from Spain and became a nation in 1816, its leaders decided to name it for this metal. At first, they were going to use the Spanish word for silver—*plata*—and call it Tierra del Plata ("land of silver"), but then decided in favor of the Latin word for the metal—*argentun*.

ASIA ■ Asia, the largest continent on Earth, gets its name from *asu,* a Sanskrit word meaning "dawn." In Sanskrit, the language of ancient India, the people were referring to the fact that the sun always rose from the land to the east of them.

ASSASSIN ■ The word *assassin* had its origins in Iran nine centuries ago, during the Christian Crusades. At that time, a secret Muslim sect lived in the mountains north of Tehran and on occasion descended upon the city to murder religious and political opponents, especially anyone connected with the Crusades. Because the cultists smoked hashish to fortify their courage before attacking, they came to be known as *hashashin*. In 1090, they changed the spelling of the word and established the Order of Assassins.

ASTROS, Houston (baseball) ■ The Houston Colt .45's joined the National League in 1962. During this period, the Colts, as they were usually referred to, played in a temporary facility located in what is now the parking lot of the Astrodome. Known as Colt Field, it was a miserable place: Fans and players alike cooked in stifling heat and humidity while being buzzed and bitten by humongous mosquitoes. In 1965, when the Colts moved into the Astrodome, the first enclosed, air-conditioned ballpark of its kind, the team named themselves after their new stadium and became the Astros.

ATLAS ■ According to Greek mythology, a giant named Atlas was given the job of holding the world on his shoulders. In 1538, Gerardus Mercator, a geographer, published the first book of maps of the world. Because its cover was illustrated with a picture of the mythological giant holding up the world, people referred to it as an "atlas." And so did publishers—and purchasers—of subsequent volumes of maps, many of which depicted a rendition of Atlas.

Aunt Jemima® Pancake Mix ■ In 1889, Charles Rutt, a Missouri newspaper reporter, came up with the idea of a ready-made pancake mix. He packaged the mix in brown paper bags and sold it to grocers. Despite its high quality, people weren't buying it.

One evening, Rutt attended a local vaudeville show. The act he liked best included a song entitled "Aunt Jemima," about a woman who was a great cook. In a sudden moment of inspiration, Rutt decided to name his flopping product Aunt Jemima Pancake Mix, after the song. And on the package would appear "Aunt Jemima's" picture—a lady in an apron and red bandanna, traditional garb of the finest southern cooks.

AUSTRALIA ■ During the 1500s, explorers were searching for a mysterious continent that they believed lay south of Asia. The continent was known as *Terra Australis Incognita*, a Latin term meaning "Unknown South Land."

In 1606, a Dutch navigator named Willem Jansz became the first known European to sight and explore the land, which he named New Holland.

For more than a century, it was not known if the landmass was a continent or two large islands. Captain James Cook explored the land's east coast in 1770; and from 1801 to 1803, a British navigator named Flinders sailed around it, proving it was a continent, the *Terra Australis* of ancient legend. By the 1820s, *Australia* became the generally accepted name for the continent.

> *The term aborigines is commonly understood to mean "the native inhabitants of Australia." Actually, the term may be applied to the original inhabitants of any region. The Latin phrase ab origine means "from the origin"; thus, an aborigine is one who has inhabited a place "from the beginning."*

Avon® ■ In 1886, D. H. McConnell was a door-to-door book salesman. To keep from having doors slammed in his face, he handed out little bottles of perfume. Book sales were hardly brisk, but the perfume was a big hit. McConnell switched from books to perfume as his door-to-door offering. Cash started coming in—enough for McConnell to start the California Perfume Company. On the 50th anniversary of the company, McConnell changed its name to Avon because of his admiration for Shakespeare, who was born in England in the town of Stratford-on-Avon.

BADMINTON ■ The game of badminton was originally called shuttlecocks. The name was changed to badminton around 1870.

At that time, there lived an English duke who loved sports, especially the game of shuttlecocks. Almost every weekend, the duke invited his friends over to play the game at his home, a mansion called Badminton House. Little by little, the game took on the name of the place where it was such a popular pastime.

Barbie® doll ■ The Barbie doll was inspired by and named after twelve-year-old Barbie Handler. In the summer of 1958, she made her own paper dolls by clipping pictures of models from magazines. Then she cut out a glamorous wardrobe of different dresses, skirts, blouses, and shoes. With a little tape and glue, she could dress the models in any way she wanted.

Her parents, Ruth and Elliot Handler (and artist Harold Mattson) were the co-owners and founders of the Mattel Toy Company. Ruth Handler wondered if her daughter's idea could be turned into a marketable toy. A few months later, Ms. Handler had a Barbie doll kit ready for sale. It consisted of a full-figured plastic doll and a stylish wardrobe. Instead of glue, the items of clothing were attached by means of snaps and buttons (and later by Velcro).

Barbie, the first dress-up figure that wasn't a baby doll, made her debut in 1959—and was a tremendous overnight success. Three years later, Ruth Handler created a male sidekick for Barbie, a teenage guy named Ken. As a doll, he's Barbie's boyfriend. In real life, he's Barbie Handler's brother. You see, Ruth and Elliot Handler also had a son. His name was Ken.

BASEBALL ■ The game began in England, around the year 1800. At first, it was called rounders, and then town ball. Runs were called aces. The players were called scouts. The batter was called a striker, and the pitcher a thrower.

In town ball, there were no bases. Instead, four-foot-high wooden stakes were used to show the runner's path.

In 1840, because so many players were injured by collision with them, the stakes were discarded in favor of sacks filled with sand. The expression "run to your stake" was abandoned for "run to your base." And *town ball* thus became *base ball*.

BASKETBALL ■ When it was invented in 1891 by teacher James Naismith, his students loved the game so much, they wanted to call it Nai-

Cagers—that's what pro basketball players used to be called. Early on, most courts were enclosed with chicken wire or other see-through fencing. The reason: to keep fans off the court and to prevent balls from going up into the stands and being stolen.

smithball. And that's what it would have been named except for one person—James Naismith. "No, gentlemen," said the inventor, "I prefer it be called basketball."

Batman® ■ Cartoonist Bob Kane created Batman in 1939, writing all the stories and doing all but a fraction of the drawings. In interviews over the years, he has told fans that his inspiration came from three sources: Zorro, the Mexican folk hero; a sketch by Leonardo da Vinci of a man trying to fly with batlike wings; and a silent mystery movie titled *The Bat Whispers*. The movie, which also inspired the name *Batman,* is about a crazed killer who lives in an old, dark mansion. In Kane's stories, Batman is a crime fighter, not a killer. In 1941, Batman picked up a sidekick, Robin, the Boy Wonder. Wrote the creator: "In my subconscious mind [when I was a kid] I longed to be like Robin Hood."

Batman and Robin lived in Gotham, which is a name for New York City created by 19th-century author Washington Irving. In Gotham, the Dynamic Duo fights a never-ending war with a gaggle of bad guys, such as the Riddler, Catwoman, and the Penguin.

BAYONET ■ A *bayonet* is a long, spearlike knife that can be attached to the barrel of a rifle for hand-to-hand combat. The weapon was named after Bayonne, France, where it was invented in the early 17th century. Initially, bayonne daggers, as they were known, had long, ramrodlike handles that went down the muzzle of a musket (a rather awkward arrangement for a soldier wanting to fire the weapon!). At the end of the 17th century, the French invented the socket bayonet. This made it possible for the rifle to be fired with the bayonet firmly secured in place—but where it belonged, outside the barrel.

BAZOOKA ■ In 1920, radio humorist Bob Burns made a crude musical instrument out of a twenty-inch piece of pipe and a rolled-up wand of paper. Burns called it a bazooka because of the sound it made. During World War II, a rocket launcher was developed by the U.S. Army, one that not only looked like an oversized version of Burns's bazooka but also, when fired, made a similar sound.

BEACH BOYS, The ■ In high school in California, the group was first known as Kenny & the Cadets, Carl & the Passions, and then the Pendletones.

Riding in their car one day in 1961, the five musicians heard their first song, "Surfin'," played on the radio and then learned that the name of their group had been officially changed to the Beach Boys. Executives at Capitol Records had picked the name on their own. Not until the DJ announced it did the Beach Boys know who they were!

BEATLES ■ The most popular rock group of the 20th century (together from 1962 to 1970) was known in its early years as the Quarrymen, Johnny and the Moondogs, the Rainbows, and the Silver Beatles. John Lennon, one of the four band members, pushed for changing the name to the Beatles. Lennon: "I liked the play on words, ya know, and it sounded kinda funky." The play on words is the suggestion of a musical "beat" and an insect (beetle) in the same name—Beatle.

Ben-Gay® ■ The menthol-based sore-muscle balm was developed in 1905 by a French pharmacist, Jules Bengué, who named the product after himself. To make the name easier for customers to pronounce, he adopted a phonetic spelling—Ben-Gay.

Betty Crocker® ■ In 1921, the Washburn Crosby Co. (the forerunner of General Mills) was receiving hundreds of letters a week asking for baking tips. To give responses a personal touch, the company created a fictional baker named Betty Crocker. The surname *Crocker* was chosen to honor the recently retired company director, William Crocker. And *Betty,* it was agreed, just sounded "warm and friendly."

For the first fifteen years after she was named, Betty was faceless. When she was given a face in 1936, it was not that of one woman but of many. An artist was hired, and he assembled all the women who worked in the company's Home Service Department to sit for the portrait. The result, stated the president, "blended all the ladies' nicest, homiest features into an official likeness."

Bic® ■ It took Frenchman Marcel Bich two years to do it, but in 1949, he invented the world's first ballpoint pen. Using the first three letters of his last name, he christened it Bic, and in 1950 he opened a large factory to produce the pens. They worked extremely well, cost only 29¢, and had a good, short, and easy-to-remember name. (In France today, *bic* is a synonym for *ballpoint pen*.)

The growth of the company has been astonishing. In 1953, Marcel Bich sold 10,000 Bic pens a day; three years later, the figure was 350,000; and now, 14 million Bic pens are sold daily!

BILLBOARD ▪ In 1839, the British Parliament passed a law forbidding the random placement of advertising bills and posters on fences, buildings, and lampposts. To get around the law, advertisements were put on stationary boards, which came to be known as billboards.

BILLIARDS ▪ Billiards and pool are played with similar rules and equipment. The name *billiards* comes from an archaic French word *villiart,* meaning "a stick." Then, as now, billiards was often a betting game in which players competed for all the money thrown into a pot. The French had a slang term for money wagered in this way. They called it the *poule,* meaning "hen."

King Louis XIV of France made billiards popular. The king had indigestion; the remedy, suggested the royal physician, was "light exercise after meals." Louis tried billiards. Not only did it give him royal relief, but the king also became an avid player. Following his example, people all over Europe started taking up the sport.

Since this French word is pronounced *pool,* English speakers adopted this phonetic spelling and began using it as the name of the game. The long, slender stick used for knocking the ball around is called a *cue,* another French slang word, this one meaning "tail."

BIRDS EYE® Frozen Foods ▪ Legend has it that centuries ago, an English queen was out for a walk in the countryside when she was suddenly attacked by a hawk. A soldier stepped forward and shot an arrow through the eye of the attacking bird. For his deed, the man was known from then on as Birds Eye.

In 1910, a distant relative of the soldier, Clarence "Bob" Birdseye, went on an expedition to Canada. While there, he discovered that fish and caribou meat

quick-frozen in the dry Arctic air were still fresh and tender when thawed out and cooked months later.

It took Birdseye eight long years before he began putting his knowledge to work. In 1926, he launched the Birdseye Seafoods Company in New York. Ten years later, after adding vegetables to his line of products, Clarence Birdseye sold the company to General Foods. They kept the original name but separated the words—*Birds Eye.*

BLACKMAIL ■ Today, *blackmail* means to "extort money," usually by threatening to reveal embarrassing secrets.

The term originated in Scotland in the 15th century, a time when *mail* meant "taxes"—money that Scottish farmers had to pay to the owners of the land they worked. The taxes could be paid in silver, also known as white mail. Or they could be paid in produce and livestock—black mail.

Greedy landlords preferred black mail. By estimating the value of the goods as low as possible, they could get even more out of the farmers than the cash amount of the taxes.

BLINDMAN'S BLUFF ■ This children's party game is a carryover from an extremely cruel medieval amusement known by the same name. When a banquet was held at the local castle, blind beggars would assemble at the gates in hopes of being chosen to star in the after-dinner "entertainment." Each guest picked a servant and wagered on him or her to be agile enough to escape being touched by the blind man. To make things even more difficult for the poor fellow, he was whirled in circles before being let loose to grope around dizzily, trying to tag servants as they raced around, laughing and making noises to attract (and distract) him. The last untagged person was the winner. As for the blind man, he was rewarded with a meal and a few coins for all the "fun" had at his expense.

BLOCKBUSTER ■ *Blockbuster* began as a slang war term used by British aviators during World War II. To them, a *blockbuster* was a five-to-eight-thousand-pound-bomb—one with enough explosive power to completely bust up a city block.

By the next decade, admen referred to movies that were big hits as blockbusters (which are definitely preferable, in movieland slang, to bombs!).

BLUE BLOOD ■ *Blue blood* is a term for a person of royal descent. The name came about because aristocrats in some European countries had very fair skin and their veins could be seen clearly.

During the Middle Ages, Spanish monarchs and aristocrats took the notion to the extreme. Wanting to appear more royal than others, they painted blue, veinlike lines on their hands, faces, and necks.

BLURB ■ A *blurb* is a short advertisement, especially one that appears on a book jacket. The term supposedly came into being in 1907 when author Gelett Burgess adorned the cover of one of his novels with a picture of a make-believe person he called Miss Blinda Blurb.

BOBBY PIN ■ Wigs were a *big* deal in 17th-century Europe—some of them were as much as four feet tall! Before being put on, the person's real hair had to be "bobbed"— pinned tightly to the head. The U-shaped wire pins that kept the heavy wigs from falling off were dubbed bobbing pins—eventually shortened to bobby pins.

BOND, JAMES ■ Ian Fleming, author of the best-selling James Bond series, took the name of the main character, a handsome special agent, from the author of one of his favorite books, *Birds of the West Indies,* by James Bond.

BONFIRE ■ During the reign of King Henry VIII of England (1491–1547) many people were put to death by being burned alive at the stake. When one of these hideous executions took place, people from all over came to watch—and they even turned the event into a kind of weird celebration. Bone fires—that's what they were called, since nothing was left of the victim but charred bone. When this gruesome practice came to an end, *bone fires* became *bonfires,* designating a giant fire set as a focus for a celebration (such as bonfires the night before football games).

BOWIE, DAVID ■ In 1962, a fifteen-year-old English kid named David Robert Jones formed his first band—the Konrads. A year later, he quit school, took a job at an ad agency, and continued performing with his fellow wannabe rock stars. As his career started taking off, David realized he had a problem: his name was already taken—by David (Davy) Jones, the popular lead singer of the Monkees. At first he called himself David Jay, but then on September 16,

Why does David Bowie have such unusual-looking eyes? He has a condition called anisocoria, the medical term for unequal pupils. In 1962, at the age of fourteen, a school friend accidentally hit him in the eye during an argument over a girl. As a result, one of his pupils remains permanently open, which gives his eyes their unique appearance.

1965, he officially changed his name to David Bowie. Why *Bowie?* The name of the knife had an intriguing, ominous sound to the former Mr. Jones.

BOWIE KNIFE ■ Many people think that Jim Bowie, the famous Texas revolutionary, made the first bowie knife. He didn't. Actually, James Black, an Arkansas blacksmith, made it in 1825. He created it from a large metal file, working from a design by Rezin Bowie, Jim Bowie's brother. The huge knife (nicknamed "the Arkansas Toothpick") was a gift from Rezin to Jim, who made the knife famous, carrying it with him until the day he died—March 6, 1836, at the Alamo.

BOXING ■ The name for this sport came about as a joke, as a playful use of language. In 17th-century England, the word *box* was a synonym for *gift.* When fighters battled with their fists, they exchanged boxes. The boxes, though, were not gifts of love; they were punches thrown at each other.

Boxing matches were first held in a ring—a circle drawn in the dirt. In 18th-century England, fans would sometimes get so wild and crazy, they'd jump into the ring and join in on the action. In the 1740s, to prevent this, the ring was made square, enclosed with ropes, and raised six feet off the ground—where it remains today.

BRASSIERE ■ In 1907, a writer for *Vogue* magazine created the name *brassiere* for the then-new undergarment. Though he didn't know it, the word *brassiere* actually referred to a jacket worn by a baby. The term derives from the French word *bras,* meaning "arm," descriptive of the fact that the baby's brassiere was a sleeveless, biblike little jacket.

BREAKFAST CEREAL ■ Ceres was the Roman goddess of grain, and it's from her name that we get the word *cereal.* And why is the first meal of the day called breakfast? One of the meanings of the word *fast* is "to eat nothing for a period of time." In the morning, we break the fast—often with a bowl of cereal!

BROWNS, Cleveland (NFL) ■ The original name of the Cleveland football team was the Panthers, selected in a newspaper contest in 1946. The winner got one thousand dollars. However, Art McBride, the Panthers owner, soon found himself in trouble with the owner of another local team called the Panthers—who demanded a large sum for the use of the name. McBride refused; instead, he changed the team's name to the Browns, after their first coach, Paul Brown.

Other than the Browns, no other pro football team was named after a person, let alone the team's coach.

In 1996, the team's new owner, Art Modell, moved it to Baltimore. But he had to leave the name *Browns,* the team colors, and the team's history in Cleveland. The Cleveland Browns were reborn (in a new stadium) in 1999. As for the Baltimore team, they became the Ravens.

BULLDOZER ■ Today, a *bulldozer* is a giant earth-moving machine. Originally, it was the name of a radical political group. Bulldozers were Southerners still fighting the North, usually politically, after the Civil War. They were known for appearing to doze off during meetings and then jumping up and raging like bulls when sensitive issues were raised.

In the first half of the 20th century, heavy machinery began to be used on southern farms. Recalling the name of the political group, they were dubbed "bulldozers." The name was an appropriate one. Like the people in the old Bulldozer political group of the South, they moved slowly but could come at you with the power of a bull.

BUNKER HILL ■ The Battle of Bunker Hill (Boston, 1775), the first major conflict of the American Revolution, was actually fought on nearby Breed's Hill. Revolutionary officers and their units were told to fortify Bunker Hill. Instead, deciding it was a better position from which to fight, they took their places on Breed's Hill, a little over a mile away. And it was there that the famous battle took place.

Bunker Hill was used during the battle to station most of the American reinforcements.

The British charged Breed's Hill three times. During the first two charges, they were slaughtered and driven back. The third time, the Revolutionaries were out of gunpowder and had to retreat.

The British suffered 1,000 casualties; the Americans had 400.

Today, Breed's Hill is a national monument—and still is known as Bunker Hill. As for the real Bunker Hill, it's covered by suburban sprawl.

BUS ■ The word is an abbreviation of *omnibus,* Latin for "everybody vehicle." The first bus began operating in 1823 in France. It was a sixteen-seat horse-drawn coach that took customers from the center of town to a bathhouse owned by the bus company.

CAMPBELL SOUP COMPANY ■ In 1869, two men in Camden, New Jersey—Joseph Campbell, a fruit merchant, and his friend Abe Anderson, an icebox manufacturer—started the Joseph A. Campbell Preserve Co., which sold everything from canned jelly to canned meats. Because 10¢ cans of soup were their hottest-selling item, Joseph and Abe changed the name to the Campbell Soup Company.

CANADA ■ In the 16th century, while Jacques Cartier was exploring North America, he came to an Iroquoian village. In French, he asked the chief the name of the country he was in, gesturing with his arms to help convey what he meant. The chief thought the Frenchman was pointing to the village, a collection of longhouses and other structures. *"Kanata,"* said the chief, using a word meaning "a cluster of huts, a village." Pleased with himself, Cartier later wrote about his discovery of "Canada."

CANARY ISLANDS ■ The islands did not get their name from canary birds; it was the other way around.

In the 15th century, Spanish explorers found great numbers of vicious wild dogs living on a group of uncharted and unnamed islands off the northern coast of Africa. The explorers could have given the islands a Spanish name—such as *Islas de los Perros* (Islands of the Dogs); instead, they used the Latin word for "dog," *canis,* from which was derived Canary Islands.

The explorers also noted that there were crowds of small yellow birds to be found. The birds were named after the islands and called canaries.

CANDIDATE ■ The word comes from the Latin *candidatus,* meaning "clothed in white," because those who sought office in Rome wore white robes. Back in Roman times, the word suggested someone who was spotless, clean, and above mudslinging!

CANTALOUPE ■ Europeans first became acquainted with this type of melon when it was brought from its native Armenia to Cantalupo, Italy. At the time, Cantalupo was the country residence of the pope. The pope's fondness for the melon resulted in the name by which it is known today.

OTHER FOODS NAMED AFTER THEIR PLACE OF ORIGIN

1. BOLOGNA (or baloney)—Bologna, Italy
2. CHAMPAGNE—the Champagne region of France
3. CHEDDAR CHEESE—Cheddar, England
4. HAMBURGER—Hamburg, Germany
5. LIMA BEANS—Lima, Peru
6. MOCHA COFFEE—Mocha, Yemen (southwest Asia)
7. PARMESAN CHEESE—Parma commune, Italy
8. SELTZER WATER—Selters, Germany
9. TABASCO SAUCE—Tabasco River and state, Mexico
10. TANGERINE—Tangier, Morocco

CAP ■ A *cappan* was a cone-shaped straw rain hat worn by English peasants during the Middle Ages. From the name of this nutty hat, we get the word *cap*.

CAPE OF GOOD HOPE ■ The Cape of Good Hope, at the southern tip of Africa, is known for its monstrous waves and terrifying currents. Bartholomeu Dias of Portugal, the first European to sight it (in 1488), named it Cabo Tormentoso, or "Cape of Storms."

King John II of Portugal changed the name to *Cabo de Boa Esperanca,* or "Cape of Good Hope." The reason? By sailing around Africa, Dias had found a waterway from Europe to Asia. This opened up vast new possibilities for trade and exploration, offering people *hope* for a better world. Besides, it was good PR. The Portuguese government didn't want to scare off sailors by letting them know that the trip around Africa involved heading straight into a hellish area called the Cape of Storms.

CARDINALS, Arizona (NFL) ■ The Cardinals are the oldest team in continuous operation in pro football history—and they've gone through the most name changes. They started out in 1898 as the Morgan Athletic Club of Chicago, a semipro team. A few years later, the owner bought used jerseys from the University of Chicago. He described the faded maroon clothing as "Cardinal red," and the team, then playing at 61st and Racine Streets, became the Racine Street Cardinals. In 1920, the club called itself the Chicago Cardinals and joined the league of teams that would eventually become the NFL. Forty years later, in 1960, they took a hike—and became the St. Louis Cardinals. In 1988, they took off again: The team went to Arizona and became the Phoenix Cardinals. And now, so as to represent the state rather than just its capital city, they're the Arizona Cardinals.

CARIBBEAN ■ The Caribbean gets its name from the Caribs, a people who have long inhabited the eastern islands of the region. At the time of the discovery, during the 1490s, the Caribs were cannibals. They sacrificed prisoners taken in battle, then (usually after cooking) had them for dinner.

CARNATION®️ Condensed Milk ■ In 1889, grocer E. E. Stuart of Kent, Washington, decided he was going to do something new: offer condensed milk in his grocery store. First he needed to think of a name for it. One day he passed a tobacconist's shop with a sign that had a flowery circle of cigars around the word *carnation*. It was a stupid name for a tobacco shop, decided Stuart, but just perfect for his new milk!

CARS ■ AUDI®️ • The Horch—that's the original name of the Audi. The car was invented by August Horch in Germany in 1909.

Horch lost control of the company for a while. When he got it back, he found that, for legal reasons, he could no longer name the car after himself. Cleverly, he translated his name, Horch, which in German means "hear," into Latin for "hear"—*audi*.

BMW®️ • Founded in 1916 in Germany, the Bavarian Motor Works, now a luxury car company, originally made aircraft engines. During World War I, BMW engines powered the planes flown by the ace German pilot the Red Baron.

BUICK® • David Dunbar Buick of Detroit started out as a plumber, went into the plumbing supplies business, and then decided to make and sell his own car design.

CADILLAC® • The Cadillac Motor Car Company of Detroit produced its first car in 1903, taking its name from the Frenchman who founded Detroit in 1701, Antoine de Cadillac.

In 1910, Cadillac offered the first "closed-bodied" cars. The self-starter, introduced on 1912 Cadillacs, eliminated the need to turn a hand crank to get the motor running.

CHEVROLET® • Frenchman Louis Chevrolet was a bicycle maker and race-car driver. In the early 1900s, he went to America to race Fiats. Louis stayed, and invented the Chevrolet.

The well-known trademark of Chevrolet cars came into being in a rather unusual way. William Durant, Louis Chevrolet's partner, created the trademark while traveling in France. In a hotel room in Paris,

In the 1920s in Maryland, there were "Chevy houses"—homes that came complete with a new Chevy in the driveway.

In 1924, Chevrolet became the first company to offer radios in its cars.

Gulf opened the first drive-in gas station in Pittsburgh in 1913.

he was attracted by the chevronlike pattern of the wallpaper. He ripped off a small sample and took it back to the United States. Within a short period of time, this wallpaper pattern had become the signature design for Chevrolets.

The Chrysler Corporation built more than 25,000 tanks during World War II.

CHRYSLER® • Walter Percy Chrysler was a big guy. At a young age, in 1912, he went to work at the Buick Motor Co. In 1920, he started his own company. Because he was such a big man, he found most cars to be uncomfortably small. His cars— Chryslers—were designed extra large.

DODGE® • Brothers John and Horace Dodge opened a machine shop in 1901 and built parts for the Olds Motor Company. In 1914, they started their own car company. From the beginning, they decided to focus on making inexpensive cars "that the average family can afford."

FERRARI® • Enzo Ferrari was born in 1898 in Italy. He saw his first auto race at the age of ten, could drive by the time he was thirteen, and was competing in auto races by the age of twenty. Before World War II, he built a few sports cars bearing his own name. But not until 1946, after the end of the war, did large-scale, commercial production of Ferraris begin.

FORD® • Henry Ford, an ambitious American inventor, named his company after himself. And his first car was called the Model T. What does the *T* stand for? Mr. Ford failed nineteen times to produce the car he was trying to create. His twentieth effort was successful—and *t* is the twentieth letter of the alphabet.

Henry Ford invented assembly-line production. A Model T Ford could be assembled in ninety-three minutes!

The Ford Motor Co. gave the station wagon its name and turned out the first of these vehicles in 1929, selling it for $650.

Ford tried making a car body out of a soybean-based plaster. It smelled so bad that it had to be scrapped.

In 1955, executives at the Ford Motor Company asked poet Marianne Moore to come up with a name for a new model of automobile they were developing. Among her many strange suggestions: the Turcotingo, the Pastelogram, the Mongoose Civique, the Resilient Bullet, and the Intelligent Whale. (The car, released in 1958, ended up being named the Edsel—after Henry's son, Edsel Ford. Large and flashy, the Edsel was introduced at a time when people wanted more economical cars and ended up being the automotive flop of the decade.)

HONDA® • Founded by Soichiro Honda of Japan in 1948, the Honda Motor Cycle Company had humble beginnings. Working out of a small shed, Mr. Honda produced the company's first vehicle—a motorized bike on an ordinary bicycle frame. For the first few years, surplus army engines—left over from World War II— were used.

In 1989, Mr. Honda became the first Asian inducted in the U.S. Automotive Hall of Fame.

JAGUAR® • No kidding, Lyons invented Jaguars.

In 1934, William Lyons designed the car. It seems natural that he would have named it the Lyon. Instead, he made up a list of five hundred fast-moving animals. For no particular reason, *jaguar* appealed to him the most.

JEEP® • When first introduced by the army during World War II, they were known as General Purpose vehicles. For a while, they were referred to as G.P.s. Then the letters were slurred together and became the word *Jeep*.

MAZDA® • In 1921, Japanese businessman Jujiro Matsuda, the twelfth son of a fisherman, fiddled around with his name and turned it into *Mazda* (which means "god of light" in Japanese).

Karl Benz led the way in the early days of the auto industry. Ironically, he was number 1 in another category too: He had the first auto accident in recorded history! One day in Germany in 1885, while test-driving his Benz Patent Motor Wagon, he missed the gate into his yard and crashed into a wall.

MERCEDES-BENZ® • The Mercedes-Benz is partly named after a young girl. The *Benz* in the name is for Karl Benz, a German pioneer of gas engines and motor-driven vehicles. *Mercedes* was the name of a ten-year-old girl, Mercedes Jellinek, whose father was a heavy investor in Mr. Benz's company.

MERCURY® • This make of car (and planet and metallic element) is named after Mercury, who, in Roman mythology, was the speedy messenger boy for the other gods.

(See Ford, page 24.)

Edsel Ford, the son of Henry Ford, loved to read Roman and Greek mythology. In 1938, knowing that his father had a new make of cars coming out, he suggested the name Mercury.

MITSUBISHI® • The name *Mitsubishi* means "three stars" in Japanese. The company has been in operation since the 19th century; and during World War II, it manufactured many of Japan's war planes, including the famous Zero fighter.

MUSTANG® • Before Mustangs started rolling off production lines in 1964, other names considered for it were Allegro, Mina, XT-Bird, Median, Colt, Bronco, and Torino (some of which ended up as names for other cars). The name comes from a Spanish word for "wild horse"—*mestengo*.

PONTIAC® • The automobile is named after the city of Pontiac, Michigan, which itself is named after a famous Native American of the Ottawa tribe, Chief Pontiac. The company started out building wagons, and then, in 1907, produced its first car, the Oakland, which evolved into the Pontiac.

PORSCHE® • The Porsche is named after Ferdinand Porsche, who designed many other cars (including the Mercedes-Benz and Volkswagen). Porsche was a friend of Adolf Hitler. During World War II, people enslaved by the Nazis built both the Volkswagen and other vehicles designed by Porsche.
(See Volkswagen®, page 27.)

ROLLS-ROYCE® • The son of an impoverished miller, Henry Royce of England worked as a newspaper boy at the age of ten and was a self-taught engineer by nineteen. One day in 1903, he bought a secondhand French car. Named the Decaulville, the thing was hard to start; and once it got going (at 4 or 5 mph), it rattled and vibrated and overheated—and stalled. Henry figured he could build a much better car. He did. Working almost alone, he hand-built a small fleet of Royces. The ride they gave—and their sales—were wonderful.

Charles Rolls was one of the fastest race-car drivers of his time. In 1903, he set a world land speed record of 93 mph. Rolls died in 1910 in an airplane accident.

Charles Rolls was the exact opposite of Henry Royce; the only similarity was that both young men were fascinated by cars and wanted to make them better. The son of an aristocrat, Rolls returned in a new car from completing his college education. The first person ever to drive into Cambridge, his hometown, he soon opened CS Rolls & Co., a firm selling foreign motorcars. But then he learned that the finest cars of all were being made by Henry Royce. The two became partners. Charles Rolls handled the finances and distribution while Henry Royce actually manufactured the cars.

There was one thing that Rolls was insistent about when signing the contract. His name had to be first. The car *had* to be Rolls-Royce, not Royce-Rolls.

SAAB® • Founded in 1937, the name is an acronym made from the company's original name: Svenska Aeroplan Aktiebolaget (Swedish Airplane Company). SAAB was founded in 1937 as a manufacturer of military airplanes for the Swedish air force. In the spring of 1940, the company produced its first plane, calling it the B-17.

In 1944, the company began tinkering with the idea of making cars instead of airplanes. Over the next two years, the workers built twenty prototypes (experimental models). In 1947, the company began mass-producing the Saab-92.

TOYOTA® • Named in 1936 after Japanese inventor Sakichi Toyoda, the company (like Honda) first produced motorbikes. The *d* was changed to a *t* because *Toyoda* requires ten characters in Japanese but *Toyota* only eight—and in Japan, *8* is considered a lucky number.

VOLKSWAGEN® • Adolf Hitler conceived the idea of the Volkswagen in 1933. Designed by Ferdinand Porsche, Hitler originally named it the *KdF-Wagen (Kraft-durch-Freude-Wagen)*, which translates as the "Strength-Through-Joy Car." This rather strange name was later changed to Volkswagen, meaning "People's Car," because it was a car that almost anyone could afford.

(See Porsche®, page 26.)

VOLVO® • First manufactured in 1926, the name of this Swedish car is Latin. *Volvo,* in Latin, means "I roll." Originally, this didn't apply to the car but to the part of the factory that produced ball bearings for the vehicle. The two inventors of the car, Gustaf Larson and Assar Gabrielsson, spent much of their time in the area, where the constant *click* and *clack* of the steel ball bearings rolling around could always be heard.

CASKET ■ Caskets were invented in Europe shortly before Columbus sailed to America in 1492. At first, they didn't hold dead bodies; a casket originally was a small metal box for holding jewels, money, and valuable documents.

In Britain today, a *casket* is still a money box. But in America, the word has gone through a strange change of meaning. During the Civil War, people who wanted to avoid a term as blunt and unpleasant as *coffin* used *casket* instead. The famous author Nathaniel Hawthorne attacked this usage, complaining that it sounded idiotic to use a word that "is suggestive of a man being buried in a little jewelry case." Despite his objections, Americans forgot the real meaning of *casket* and began using it exclusively as a term for "a burial box."

Chanel® No. 5 ■ France introduced this now-famous perfume on the fifth day of the fifth month of 1951 because *5* was the lucky number of French fashion designer Coco Chanel, the owner of the company.

CHARGERS, San Diego (NFL) ■ The name may suggest the idea of charging into action, but that's not where it came from. The original team owner was Barron Hilton, who also owned the Carte Blanche charge-card company. For their first year of operation, 1960, they were the Los Angeles Chargers. Though they won their division that year, their fan support was dismal. In 1961, the team moved—and became the San Diego Chargers.

CHAUFFEUR ■ Down through history, the word *chauffeur* has referred to three *very* different occupations.

The first *chauffeurs* ("torchers") showed up in France in 1793. Not until 1795 were all of them finally caught and hanged. You see, *chauffeurs* were thieves, cruel ones with an especially horrible method of getting everything they wanted. After breaking into a house, they tied the owner to a chair and then forced his feet into the flames in a fireplace. Again and again, the victim was tortured in this way until the *chauffeurs* were satisfied he had told them where all his money and valuables were hidden.

In the 19th century, the word *chauffeur* reemerged in France—but with a greatly changed meaning. During this time, steamships had begun making regular voyages. Aboard English and American ships, the men who shoveled coal into the steam-producing furnaces were called stokers. On French ships, they came to be known by a slang term, one filled with dark humor and a twisted reference to the past. They were called chauffeurs.

As well as steam-powered ships, the 19th century was the era of the steam-driven car. Such vehicles tended to be especially big and fancy, and their operators had to do a lot more than just drive them. They had to stoke the engine's fire too. That is, they had to be chauffeurs.

By the 20th century, the term had come to take on its present meaning, "the driver of a (usually large and comfortable) car who takes others to their destinations."

CHESS ■ The game evolved from one played for centuries in India called chaturanga, meaning "four parts." It was a war game in which each player had four types of pieces: elephants, horses, chariots, and foot soldiers—the four basic components of an Indian army at the time.

When the game reached Europe in the Middle Ages, the pieces took on the names of the social roles common to European society. Thus, there was the king and queen, the bishops and knights, and the rook (castle). Deriving from the old French word *échecs,* the name of the game was translated as *chess,* meaning "check." The object of the game was to put the opponent's king in checkmate, a word taken from the Persian *al shah mat,* meaning "the king is dead."

In medieval chess, the king had nearly the same role and moves as today. The piece now known as the queen, however, was originally a male counselor. This was changed to vierge ("virgin") and later to regina ("queen"). The queen formerly moved only one square diagonally and was consequently the weakest piece on the board. (She was given her current great powers in the 15th century.) The bishop's scope of action used to be more limited too; he could move only two squares diagonally. The rooks (from the Indian word rukh, meaning "powerful soldier") and the knights had the same powers as they do today.

CHICAGO ■ The Indian word *chicago,* means "strong, great, powerful." The word could be used in a positive way—to describe lakes and other geographical features in the region as being "great." At the same time, it was also used in a negative way—to describe such things as the powerful stench of wild onions, skunks, and rotten meat.

> *For a time, the jazz-rock group Chicago called themselves Los Angeles!*

CHINA ■ The country is named after Emperor Ch'in, its first ruler (221–210 B.C.). Historically speaking, he gets mixed reviews. Taking the throne at the age of thirteen, Ch'in accomplished great things: He united the country, standardized its writing system, and directed the building of the Great Wall of China. For centuries, the Chinese enslaved their own people as farmers. Ch'in outlawed this and permitted farmers to own their own land.

Ch'in was also a terribly strange, vain, and cruel man. He had untold thousands butchered in order to achieve his ambitions. On his orders, his soldiers burned thousands of literary and historical documents, especially those that gave a version of the past that displeased him. He had the authors burned to death too. At the same time, he was incredibly afraid of his own death. To fool would-be assassins, he crept through underground passageways connecting his 270 palaces and slept in a different bed every night. Despite all of his odd precautions, death finally caught up with Ch'in, in 210 B.C. He was forty-nine. Worried that grave diggers, pallbearers, and other workers would come back and rob his grave, Ch'in ordered in his will that they be buried with him—alive. This was in addition to the eight thousand terra-cotta sculptures (statues) of Chinese soldiers buried with him to guard him in death! Each member of this stone army has unique facial and physical features, and each has the weapons and uniform of his particular fighting unit.

> *The "stone army" was discovered in 1970 when a crew of well diggers struck something far more unusual than water.*

CHINESE CHECKERS ■ The game was invented in England (in the 19th century), not in China, and was originally known as Alma. The confusion about the game's origin comes from the single star shape in the center of the board, which, coincidentally, resembles the star on China's flag.

CHOCOLATE ■ In 1519, Hernán Cortés, a Spanish explorer, invaded Mexico. He found that the Aztecs drank a frothy, bitter drink they called *chocolatl* (also spelled *xocolatl*) made from cacao beans. When Cortes first introduced hot chocolate to Spain in the 1520s, the drink was flavored with pepper and cinnamon. After a while, it was sweetened with sugar instead, as it is today.

CHOW ■ When English visitors were served meals in China, their hosts often said, "Gǒu," or "Chow." The travelers thought they had learned a new word for "food." What they didn't realize was that they'd been eating *gǒu*, Chinese for "dog"! Or that sometimes they'd been given a delicacy, a special kind of Chinese dog, the chow.

CHRISTMAS ■ The word means "a mass (religious service) celebrating the birth of Christ" ("Christ's Mass"). Originally, *mass* was a Latin word said at the end of the service by the priest to the congregation. It meant "You may go now."

For four hundred years after the birth of Christ, there was no such thing as Christmas. At first, Christ's Mass was not a very festive or merry occasion; rather it was a day of prayer and fasting. All of the things we associate with Christmas—gifts, Santa Claus, and decorated trees—did not come until much later.

(See Xmas, page 133.)

CHUMP ■ Today a *chump* is a foolish person, a blockhead. Originally, a *chump* was a chopping block for woodcutters.

CLEVELAND, Ohio ■ The city was named in 1796 after Moses Cleaveland, a lawyer who fought in the Revolutionary War. Why was the spelling changed? According to the Smithsonian, an 18th-century newspaper reporter dropped the first *a* so that he could cram a headline using the name into a limited space.

Coca-Cola® ■ Coca-Cola is named for two of its original ingredients—coca leaves and kola nuts. The coca-leaf derivative (cocaine) was removed from the contents in 1903.

John Pemberton, a Confederate veteran who opened a drugstore in Atlanta after the Civil War, mixed the first batch of Coca-Cola in 1886 in a three-legged iron pot in his backyard. His friend and bookkeeper, F. M. Robinson, named the drink.

The American public nicknamed the beverage Coke, much to the dismay of company executives, who launched an advertising campaign to remedy the situation. The ads insisted: "Ask for Coca-Cola by its full name; nicknames encourage substitution." Indifferent, customers continued ordering "Coke." The company, rather than fight a losing battle, did an about-face and, in 1920, patented Coke as a legal trademark.

COPS ■ In 1829, Englishman Robert Peel organized the first modern police force. The officers wore navy blue uniforms with large copper buttons. Because of the buttons, policemen were first called *coppers,* soon shortened to *cops.*

CORDUROY ■ Originally, corduroy was a fabric woven from silk, worn exclusively by the kings of France as part of their hunting costumes. From the French *corde du roi,* the name means "cloth of the king." Today, corduroy is a soft, ribbed cloth, usually made from cotton.

CORNY ■ If something is *corny,* it's dumb, lame, geeky, and simple-minded— sometimes with a touch of sentimental mushiness thrown in.

Mail-order seed catalogs of the early 1900s—that's the unlikely source of the term. In a feeble attempt to make such catalogs entertaining, the publishers threw in cartoons, stories, and jokes—most of them pathetically bad. From then on, any low-level material was said to be "straight from the corn catalog," an expression that soon became just plain "corny."

COTTON CANDY ■ Thomas Patton invented a cotton candy maker while working at a Ringling Brothers Circus in 1900. When his machine was adopted for use in other countries, the name of the spun sugar candy didn't always go with it. For example, in France, it's known as *la barbe de papa,* meaning, "papa's beard."

Cracker Jack® ■ Without a name, a combination of caramel-coated peanuts and popcorn has been around since the 1870s. In 1890, F. W. Rueckheim, a German immigrant, began packaging it in small boxes. A salesman tasted it and exclaimed, "That's crackerjack!" a slang expression of the time meaning "super!" Breaking the word in two, Rueckheim had a name for his product.

The sailor boy on the package, Jack, and his black-and-white dog, Bingo, became a company trademark in 1916. The model for Jack was Rueckheim's grandson Robert. (When Robert died, the sailor boy Cracker Jack image was carved on his tombstone.) In 1913, a prize was added to boxes of Cracker Jacks. Before that, each box contained a discount coupon for another purchase.

CROISSANT ■ In 1863, a Turkish army attacked and besieged the city of Vienna, Austria. When the soldiers and citizens of Vienna drove them off, the city's bakers created a new pastry, one that celebrated and symbolized the victory. It was in the shape of a crescent, the national emblem of the defeated Turks. *Croissant* is French for "crescent."

CROSSWORD PUZZLE ■ When Art Wynne was a little boy growing up in England, he and his grandfather loved to do word puzzles together. One of these was a rather simple game called Magic Squares.

After moving to the United States, Wynne took a job with a newspaper, the *New York World*. His main task every week was to create a Sunday entertainment supplement called *FUN,* which consisted of cartoons, stories, and puzzles. One day in December 1913, Wynn's boss told him to come up with a new word game.

Magic Squares immediately came to mind. But it was too easy, Wynne decided; the puzzle consisted simply of words that had to be arranged in such a way that they read the same down as across. Wynne changed the puzzle completely: Instead of a list of words, he gave definitions and clues; the answers did not read the same down as across; the words crisscrossed in intricate, complicated ways; and there were blackened squares built into the grid.

Mental Exercises—that was Wynne's name for his new word game. He never referred to them as "crossword puzzles." His boss at the newspaper changed the name to Word-Cross. In time, the hyphen was dropped, and the words were reversed to create the more pleasant-sounding "Crossword."

CRUSOE, ROBINSON ■ Robinson Crusoe wasn't just a character in a famous novel about a man stranded on a desert island. He was a real person named Alexander Selkirk. At the age of nineteen, Selkirk left his home in Scotland and went to sea. Off the coast of South America, Selkirk's vessel engaged two Spanish galleons in battle. Badly shot up, it limped away and anchored off the remote island of *Más a Tierra* to make emergency repairs. When the captain was ready to leave again, Selkirk was not. The sailor said he would rather be put ashore than continue on with an idiot of a captain in a leaky ship. The captain was more than willing to oblige the rash, disrespectful young man. But at the last minute, Selkirk changed his mind. Crying, he waded into the surf and begged to be taken back aboard. From the deck, the captain laughed and sailed away.

More than four years later, two British ships driven to the island by a storm rescued Selkirk. The English sailors found him to be half man, half beast. He wore a foul-smelling goatskin costume, lived in a cave, and babbled incoherently, having temporarily lost the ability to speak. Returning to Scotland, he was an odd, fearful man. On his family's property, he dug a cave into the side of a hill. And that's where he lived, with only cats as companions, venturing out now and then to eat, sometimes telling the story of his strange adventures on the island.

Robinson Crusoe is a made-up name; and so are the names Alexander Selkirk and Daniel Defoe. Both men had been in trouble with the law, the sailor for fighting and the author for his writings against the government. Selkirk's real name was Alexander Selcraig; the author's name was Daniel Foe, not Defoe.

Daniel Defoe, a penniless English author, was one of those who heard of the castaway's ordeal. The story fired his imagination. He sat down and began writing a novel. Changing the name of the story's main character, he titled his work *The Adventures of Robinson Crusoe*. It became his most famous book.

Unlike Selkirk, Crusoe was stranded on the island due to a shipwreck. And instead of turning into a half-crazed beast, Crusoe remained a dignified human being—strong, resourceful, and inventive. Published in 1719, *Robinson Crusoe* has remained a classic ever since.

CURFEW ■ In the Middle Ages, the danger of fire spreading through a village or town was very great. At a given hour of night, the town crier, a person who called out public announcements through the streets, yelled, *"Couvre feu!,"* warning all citizens to put out their fires. Our word *curfew* comes directly from the French *couvre feu,* meaning "cover the fire."

CZAR ■ The words *czar* (Russian for "emperor") and *kaiser* (German for "ruler") are both taken from the name of the most famous Roman leader, Julius *Caesar.*

DACHSHUND ■ These little dogs were first bred in Germany in the 16th century for underground warfare with badgers, burrowing animals that kill small livestock and eat crops. (In German, *dachs* means "badger" and *hund* means "dog." With their short legs and long, thin bodies, dachshunds were ideal for crawling down tunnels to flush badgers from their underground dens.

Badgers dig rapidly, easily out-distancing a man with a shovel.

DAISY ■ This flower gets its name from the fact that it opens at dawn. At first it was known as a day's eye, then slurred in common usage into the word *daisy.*

DALMATIAN ■ Not only in the United States, but around the world, these white dogs with black spots have been adopted as fire department mascots. Their name derives from where they were originally bred—Dalmatia, a region of what was once part of the country of Yugoslavia.

DANDELION ■ In France, this weed with a yellow flower was called *dent-de-lion* ("lion's tooth"), referring to the sharp leaves of the plant. In English, *dent-de-lion* mutated into *dandelion.*

DAYS OF THE WEEK ■ In ancient times, many aspects of daily life had important connections to what people saw when they looked up at the sky. Names were given to the seven mysterious objects they saw there—the sun, the moon, and the five planets visible to the naked eye. The week was divided into seven days, and each day was named

For thousands of years, seven has been considered a lucky number. Why? The reason is that people believed that there was something wonderful and magical about the seven heavenly bodies visible to the naked eye.

for one of the heavenly bodies, which people believed had magical qualities associated with their gods. The English names for days of the week came from old Anglo-Saxon words for those same seven heavenly bodies that were so important to ancient peoples.

Sunday was considered the first day of the week. Its name comes from Sunnan daeg, which means "the sun's day."

Monday comes from Monan daeg, meaning "the moon's day."

Tuesday was "Tiwe's day," so called because Tiwe was the Anglo-Saxon word for Mars, the planet named for the god of war.

Wednesday derives its name from Wodens daeg—"Woden's day." Woden (also known as Odin) was the supreme Germanic god, associated with the planet Mercury.

Thursday was once known as Thurs daeg, meaning "Thor's day." Thor was the god of thunder, also known as Jupiter.

Friday was "Frigga's day," or Frige daeg. Frigga was Thor's beautiful and powerful wife, associated with the planet Venus and considered to be the goddess of beauty, love, and fertility.

Saturday comes from Satern daeg—"Saturn's day," named for the god of agriculture.

(See Planet Names, page 90.)

DEAD SEA ■ This body of water in the Middle East is actually a lake—and the lowest point on Earth (1,300 feet below sea level). Its name couldn't be more perfect—due to its extremely high salt content, it contains no living organisms.

DEATH VALLEY ■ In 1849, a group of thirty-nine headed west in covered wagons to the goldfields of California. Among them were Juliet Brier (the only woman); her husband, John; and their three young sons. In studying their map, the travelers discovered what appeared to be a shortcut—across a desert that stretched between what is now western Nevada and eastern California. A month later, thirty-five sunken-eyed, living skeletons, with Mrs. Brier in the lead, emerged from the furnacelike hell of the place, starving and dehydrated. Most of their oxen had died and been eaten, and four original members of the group had perished. Shrunken to a mere seventy-five pounds, Juliet looked back at the scorching desert they had crossed and said, "Good-bye, Death Valley."

DENNIS THE MENACE ■ There really was a Dennis the Menace. His name was Dennis Ketcham, and he was the inspiration for his cartoonist father, Hank Ketcham.

DERRICK ■ One of the most famous executions in English history was that of the Earl of Essex. Young, handsome, and intelligent, the earl was loved by the commoners; but then, in 1601, he was convicted of treason and condemned to death by Queen Elizabeth.

One icy morning, Essex was led to the block to be beheaded with an ax. By the strangest of coincidences, his executioner, a fellow named Derrick, was a man whose life had been saved by Essex only months before. Weeping, Derrick begged Essex to forgive him for what he was about to do.

Essex not only forgave Derrick, he consoled him—and then lowered his head to the block. Derrick struck a heavy blow with his ax. It was poorly aimed, and two more efforts were needed before the head was finally severed from the body.

Friends and admirers of Essex attacked Derrick and almost killed him. Rescued by soldiers, he lived to perform hundreds more executions, most of them hangings. Derrick became so notorious an executioner that his name became another word for *gallows*.

In the 19th century, a type of crane was invented for drilling for oil. The device was a tower of wood and iron, a skeleton framework that resembled a gallows—or, as it was more popularly known, derrick.

DIESEL ENGINE ■ In 1892, a young German engineer named Rudolf Diesel published an article about a new internal combustion engine he had invented. The engine was especially powerful, he explained, and thus would be extremely well suited for use in large vehicles such as "trucks, locomotives, and ships." What were first known as Diesel's engines quickly became popular. To his disappointment, however, Rudolf was never able to interest anyone in his other project—solar-powered engines.

DINOSAUR ■ Dinosaur fossils had been known for centuries as dragon bones. The term *Dinosauria* was invented by Sir Richard Owen in 1842, and from this word evolved *dinosaur*. The name means "terrible

Crocodiles are dinosaurs' closest living relatives; birds are their living descendants.

lizard" in Greek. It's a largely inappropriate name. For one thing, these creatures were not lizards. Also, most weren't very big or very terrible. Some were the size of cats, lived in trees, and really weren't dangerous at all—unless you were a plant!

Dixie® cups ■ Until early in the 20th century, people drank from "common cups," an arrangement that consisted of a bucket of water and a tin sipper. Realizing this was very unsanitary, in 1908, Hugh Moore of the United States invented a watercooler—a porcelain vending machine that dispensed a single drink of pure, chilled water for a penny. The paper cup, also his invention, was free. Health Kups— that's what he first called them. Then he changed the name to one he liked better: Dixie cups, naming them after the Dixie Doll Company, whose office was down the hall of the building where Mr. Moore worked.

Paper cups became increasingly popular as American cities and states began outlawing the use of sippers in 1909.

Moore also invented the ice-cream cup. With a pull-up lid and a disposable wooden spoon, they were the first single-serving packages of the treat.

Luther Haws and Halsey Taylor of Berkeley, California, invented the drinking fountain in the early 1900s. Taylor came up with the idea after his father died from drinking typhoid-contaminated water.

DOBERMAN PINSCHER ■ Ludwig Dobermann was a tax collector and dog breeder. In 1890, he developed a new breed of guard dog to protect and assist him when he went house to house on his rounds. Dobermann's route was in Pinzgau— an area in northern Austria, then part of Germany. *Pinscher* may come from that word, but its history is also linked to a kind of terrier, as well as to the German word *pinch,* associated with how a dog's ears and tail were cropped.

DODGERS, Los Angeles (baseball) ■ Long before moving from Brooklyn to L.A., members of a baseball team known as the Superbas were often seen walking to the ballpark, dodging the numerous trolley cars of the time. People began referring to the Superbas as the "trolley-dodging team." The players liked the name. Dumping Superbas, the team adopted the nickname Trolley Dodgers, which soon became just Dodgers.

DOLLAR ■ The dollar was Thomas Jefferson's idea, and he named it after the *Daler,* a German coin first minted in 1519. The Daler was, in turn, named after a small town in Czechoslovakia where similar coins were first minted.

And how did a *dollar* become a *buck*? In North America in the 1700s, the going rate for the skin of a male deer was a dollar. A male deer is called a buck—and in time a dollar was called the same thing.

> A stack of dollars one mile high would contain more than 14¼ million notes.

> According to federal law, you must be dead to get your picture on paper money.

> Martha Washington is the only woman whose likeness has appeared on a U.S. currency note (paper money). Her picture was featured on the front of the $1 silver certificate of 1886 and 1891 and on the back of the $1 silver certificate of 1896.

DRACULA ▪ In the 1890s, Irishman Bram Stoker decided to write a novel about something that had always fascinated him—vampires. At first, Stoker was going to use a make-believe main character, but during his research he stumbled upon an historical account of a man who, though not a vampire, was terribly bloodthirsty. The man was Vlad Tepes, a prince who lived during the 15th century in a castle in Transylvania (now part of Romania). Totally nuts, the prince's hobby was torturing and murdering

> Dracula's father, a vicious and clever ruler, was called Dracul, meaning "the devil" or "the dragon.

people, his specialty being the impaling of live victims on sharpened stakes. Tepes's nickname was Dracula, which means "son of the devil" or "son of the dragon."

DUD ▪ A *dud* was originally World War I American slang for a bomb that failed to go off. Now a *dud* is a party, a movie, a joke, or anything else that doesn't "go off" very well.

DUDE ▪ A wimp. A sissy—especially one who dressed in fancy, frilly clothes. That's what a *dude* used to be, back when the word first entered the English language (from France) in the 1800s.

By the 1900s, there were dude ranches in the western United States. These were places for tourists—city boys who wanted to ride horses and pretend they were fearless cowboys for a few days. At least that's how the owners of such establishments viewed their guests.

But it became clear pretty quickly that a lot of the dudes showing up really *were* tough, strong guys. By the 1950s, the word had completely reversed in meaning. Dudes had become good people—likable, respected, and accepted by the rest of the group.

DUNGAREES ■ Dungaree work pants and overalls get their name from a poor-quality cloth produced in Dungri, an impoverished area of Bombay, India.

EAGLES, Philadelphia (NFL) ■ Two owners swapped pro football teams—that's how it all started. In 1941, the owner of the Pittsburgh team traded all the players on his team for all the players on the Philadelphia team. Once in their new city, the team was named after the national bird of the United States.

In 1943, due to manpower shortages created by World War II, the Philadelphia Eagles and Pittsburgh Steelers franchises combined for one season and became the Phil-Pitt Steagles.

EDITOR ■ Today an editor is someone who helps decide whether or not to publish a book and, if so, what changes need to be made before the work goes to print.

Originally, an editor made a different kind of decision—between life and death. In the Roman Colosseum, there was always only one "editor"—the emperor.

When gladiators battled and one was overpowered, the combatant with the upper hand—perhaps with a knife to the throat of his opponent—looked to the emperor. As Editor of the Games, the emperor always took into account the wishes of the crowd. If the

Enormous canvas awnings that covered the entire arena shaded spectators at the Colosseum in ancient Rome. Raised by an intricate system of ropes and pulleys, the awnings were supported by 240 tall wooden shafts at the top edge of the stadium wall.

downed gladiator had fought bravely, the people in the stands would wave hand-kerchiefs and shout "*Mitte!*" ("Let him go!"). If the editor had been persuaded, he would then raise his thumb. Finally, the gladiator who had been spared would exit the arena through the Porta Sanavivaria, the "Gate of Life." A thumbs-down signal meant instant death.

In 2002, the Eiffel Tower welcomed its 200 millionth visitor!

EIFFEL TOWER ■ The Eiffel Tower was completed in 1889 to celebrate the one hundredth anniversary of the French Revolution. Of the seven hundred

Near the top of the tower is a suite of rooms that were once used by Gustave Eiffel.

proposals submitted in a design competition, French engineer Alexandre Gustave Eiffel's was unanimously chosen. The tower is con-structed of 7,000 tons of iron, and it's 984 feet high. Every five years it gets a new paint job—with 50 tons of paint.

For the official opening on May 1, 1931, President Herbert Hoover pressed a button in Washington, D.C., to turn on the building's lights.

EMPIRE STATE BUILDING ■ In the 1700s, George Washington nicknamed New York the Empire State. In 1931, a building 102 stories high (1,250 feet) was com-pleted in New York. Then the tallest building in the world, it was given the state's nickname.

ENGLAND and ENGLISH ■ In 500 A.D., two German tribes, the Angles and Saxons, invaded England. And amazing as it may seem, it was the German lan-guage spoken by these fierce warriors that slowly changed into the English we speak today.

In the beginning, the Angles were called the Angli. As time went by, their name changed to the Engle. The place where they lived was called Engla-land. And the language they spoke was *englisc,* which is now English.

EUROPE ■ The continent gets its name from a Greek myth in which Zeus, the supreme Greek god, falls in love with a beautiful mortal girl named Europa. To trick her, Zeus transforms himself into a bull. Europa, while picking flowers near

the seaside one day, finds herself approaching the majestic but very tame-looking animal. She pets it and then climbs playfully onto its shoulders. Suddenly, the bull rears up and races off with Europa across the sea—in the direction of what is now Europe.

EVEREST ■ Mount Everest is named after Sir George Everest, a 19th-century British surveyor who was first able to calculate and prove that it was the highest mountain in the world (29,028 feet). Prior to this, the British merely referred to it as Peak XV. To the people of Nepal, it was *Sagarmatha,* meaning "goddess of the sky."

Ex-Lax® ■ Even though it's funny, no one's joking when it comes to Ex-Lax's original name—Bo-Bo. (Imagine having to tell someone suddenly, "I need to take a Bo-Bo!")

Max Kiss invented the product, but the name produced more laughs than customers. Sales took off when Kiss changed the name to Ex-Lax, his contraction of the words *excellent laxative.*

Exxon® ■ Wasting loads of time and money, Standard Oil of New Jersey spent $100 million and three years of study in finding a new name. The name, said company executives, had to be completely new, easy to pronounce, and not mean anything in any language. With the help of a computer, ten thousand names were created. Finally, in 1973, after additional tests and surveys, *Exxon* was selected.

> If the expense of selecting the word Exxon is broken down, the cost is $20 million per letter!

FALCONS, Atlanta (NFL) ■ Purchased on June 30, 1965, one of the owner's first orders of business was to announce a contest for a team name. Many contestants suggested *Falcons,* but a schoolteacher from Griffin, Georgia, was declared the official winner. Perhaps this was because, in her contest entry letter, she wrote: "The falcon is proud and dignified, with great courage and fight. It never drops its prey. It is deadly and has a great sporting tradition."

FASCISM ■ This form of government is characterized by one-party rule, dictatorship, and oppression of minorities and opposition parties.

The word has its origins in one of Aesop's fables, a story in which sticks could easily be snapped one by one but couldn't be broken if tied together in a bundle. The moral: In union there is strength. The fable spread from Greece to Rome. There, a bundle of sticks (a *fasces*) became a symbol of unity and strength.

> *Benito Mussolini was named after Benito Juárez, the Native American president of Mexico from 1858 to 1872.*

Centuries later, when Benito Mussolini took power in Italy in 1922, he reinstated the Roman symbol and named his followers *Fascists* and his form of dictatorship *fascism.*

FENCING ■ *Fencing* is the sport of fighting with a foil or other type of sword. The term comes from the medieval English word *fens,* short for *defense.*

FERRIS WHEEL ■ Built in 1893, the Ferris wheel was named after its inventor, George Washington Ferris. The largest wheel ever built was one constructed for the World's Columbian Exposition in Chicago in 1893. The wheel was 250 feet in diameter, and each of its thirty-six cars could hold up to sixty people! This Ferris wheel was last used at the St. Louis Exhibition in 1904, after which it was torn down and sold for scrap metal.

FIRST STRING ■ This sports term originated in the 13th century among archers. Every marksman had several bowstrings, one of which was his best and favorite. Today the term *first string* refers to the best players, the first sent into the game.

FLAK ■ The metal fragments released by exploding antiaircraft shells are called flak. The word is German slang, an acronym of *Fliegerabwehrkanone,* meaning "antiaircraft cannon." The current expression "to give someone flak" means "to bombard them with complaints and criticism."

FLOUR ■ During the 19th century, the word *flower* was used as a poetic expression (and a synonym) for the word *best.* For example, a person might have said, "She is a flower of a friend." It was applied to merchandise, artwork, weapons, animals, and even to people who were "the best" in some way.

After grinding their wheat, millers carefully sifted it so that only the finest of it passed through the sieve. Reserved for the tables of the wealthy, this top-grade product was called flower of the wheat, which in time became *flour.*

FLYSWATTER ■ Schoolteacher Frank Rose of Kansas invented the flyswatter in 1909 out of a yardstick and a piece of wire screen. A flybat—that's what Mr. Rose called his invention.

Mr. Rose's invention was his contribution to a public-health crusade in Kansas in 1909. Another contribution was paper cups, invented by Hugh Moore in 1908. (See Dixie® Cups, page 39)

FORFEIT ■ *Forfeit* comes from Old French *forfait,* meaning "to do wrong." And by the way, the score of a forfeited baseball game is 9–0; softball is 7–0; and football, weirdly, is 1–0 (the strange thing being that *1*—by itself—is the only number that can never be in the final score of a football game).

FRANCE ■ During the Middle Ages, the Franks were a tough, warlike Germanic tribe. They settled in what the Angles and Saxons, two other brutal German tribes, called Franca. At the time, the nation included all of the land that is now France, Germany, and Italy.

FRANKENSTEIN ■ In 1817, five people had a contest to see who could write the most frightening horror story. One night, one of the writers, Mary Shelley, had a dream in which she saw "a pale student kneeling beside a man he had put together, a living monster made of the parts of dead bodies." Mary wrote a story based on the nightmare, won the contest, and later turned her story into the best-selling book *Frankenstein, or The Modern Prometheus*.

In the book, Dr. Frankenstein was the name of the scientist who created the monster. The monster has no name, though Dr. Frankenstein on occasion refers to him as Adam (after the biblical first man). However, in common usage, the monster has taken on the name of his creator.

GATLING GUN ■ Dr. Richard Gatling (1818–1903) was a fully licensed physician but never practiced medicine. Instead, he turned his talents to invention, especially weaponry (a curious switch from helping people to hurting them). During the Civil War (1861–1865), he invented a crank-operated machine gun that was capable of firing three hundred rounds per minute. To "sell" the weapon to the Union Army, and to demonstrate its effectiveness, Dr. Gatling set it up during a battle and hammered away at Confederate troops.

GEEK ■ In the 15th and 16th centuries, a *geek* was a carnival performer of weird, sick acts, such as biting off the heads of live chickens. Today, the word is used as a derogatory term to describe someone who just doesn't fit in.

GENIUS ■ The first-ever genius was from Persia (now Iran). In ancient Persian religion, Genius was the creative force and magical power of being. Not only people had Genius; so too did the things they made—walls, houses, streets, and so forth.

The Romans continued this belief in Genius. To them, Genius was what presided over each man—and it was all the things that made him unique and intelligent and alive. The Genius of females was Juno.

Genies, those big, supernatural beings that come out of bottles, also derive from the word genius.

Today the term *genius* refers to any person of great mental capacity.

Gerber® Baby Food ■ It all started in the kitchen of Daniel and Dorothy Gerber in the summer of 1927. Dorothy was getting tired of hand straining solid food for her seven-month-old daughter, Sally, and asked her husband to try doing the time-consuming chore. After watching him make several attempts, she pointed out that the work could probably be done easily at the Fremont Canning Company, where Dan worked. Dan, covered in strained peas and carrots, thought his wife had a good point. By early 1929, Gerber baby foods were on grocery store shelves across America.

The original Gerber Baby was Ann Turner Cook, whose picture the Gerbers began using in 1928.

GERMANY ■ In 100 B.C., several warlike tribes occupied the land to the north of Rome. The Romans called all of them Germani, though that was the name of only one tribe. In time, "the land of the Germani" became *Germany.*

GHOULS ■ Ghouls supposedly come out at night to rob graves and eat human corpses. The name, which has been around for centuries, comes from the Arabic word *ġūl,* meaning "demon of the mountains."

G.I. ■ During World War II, soldiers received everything from weapons to toiletries from the government. Such supplies were "General Issue," and that's what *G.I.* first meant. It has now also come to stand for "General Infantry."

G.I. Joe ■ In 1962, a series called *The Lieutenant* was being filmed and readied for airing on TV. Hearing of the upcoming show, a businessman by the name of Stanley Weston had a sudden inspiration: He'd make a doll-like toy for boys, a soldier that, like the fabulously successful Barbie doll, had all sorts of accessories—in this case, a rifle, backpack, helmet, and different types of uniforms.

The producer of the TV show thought it was a great idea—and paid Mr. Weston $100,000 for the rights to it. But what would the soldier/doll be named? Hundreds of ideas were suggested; all were rejected—until someone asked: "How about 'G.I. Joe'?"

The name was from a 1945 war movie entitled *The Story of G.I. Joe.* When the movie was released, it popularized a slang term for American soldiers. Fifteen years later, it was the name of the first action figure for boys.

GIANTS, San Francisco (baseball) ■ They began as the New York Mutuals. After winning a crucial game in 1886, their manager referred to them as his "big fellows," after which fans began referring to them as the "Giants." In 1957, the team headed west and became the San Francisco Giants.

Gillette® ■ Mr. King Camp Gillette was a failed author and salesman. One day a friend, William Painter, inventor of the throwaway bottle cap, suggested that Gillette develop a disposable item of some kind. Nothing clicked—until one morning he was trying to shave with a dull straight razor. Gillette later wrote: "As I stood there with the razor in my hand, my eyes resting on it as lightly as a bird settling down on its nest, the Gillette razor and disposable blade were born."

Women in prehistoric times used sharpened flints and seashells as razors. It is not known for sure if they were brave or stupid, but some women in ancient Greece rid their legs of hair with the flame from a candle or oil lamp.

Fortunately, the safety razor was named after the ecstatic Gillette and not after the engineer who, six years later, was able to produce them—William Nickerson. As a name for a shaving device, the Nickerson just doesn't cut it!

GIMMICK ■ In the United States around the turn of the 19th century, a *gimcrack* was a showy but cheap prize won at carnivals. To keep people from walking away with too many gimcracks, carnival workers had "gimmicks"—ways to trick and cheat customers (such as a hidden brake on a roulette wheel to control its stopping point). In time, a *gimmick* came to mean any device or strategy for getting the best of someone.

GIRAFFE ■ The Spanish called the animal a *jirafa*. The Romans called it a *camelopard*—because its body and long neck were like that of a camel and its spots were like those of a leopard. The Spanish won this little war of words; from the Spanish *jirafa* came the English word *giraffe*.

GLADIATOR ■ In ancient Rome, gladiators went into the arena armed with *gladiolus*,

Latin for "swords." Also deriving its name from the Latin word is the gladiola plant, which has long, swordlike leaves.

(See Editor, page 41.)

GOBI DESERT ■ While tromping around one of the biggest deserts he'd ever seen, Sven Hedin, a 19th-century explorer from Sweden, spotted some of the native inhabitants. "Hey, what's this place called?" he asked the people in Swedish, gesturing around at the sand-swept wilderness. Quite possibly thinking Sven was an idiot, they told him, "It's called a desert." (In the language of the region, *gobi* means "desert.") When he got home, Sven reported that he had discovered the Gobi desert, or what might also be called the Gobi *gobi,* or Desert desert.

GONE WITH THE WIND ■ It took Margaret Mitchell, a fiesty journalist from Atlanta, ten years to write her epic novel *Gone with the Wind,* which won the prestigious Pulitzer Prize in 1937. It was not until just prior to being cast into type that Ms. Mitchell changed the heroine's name from Pansy O'Hara to Scarlett and the title from *Tomorrow Is Another Day* to *Gone with the Wind.*

Before this, the book had seven other titles: *Tote the Weary Load, Milestones, Jettison, Ba! Ba! Black Sheep, None So Blind, Not in Our Stars,* and *The Bugles Sang True.*

The final title was inspired by a poem written in 1896 by Englishman Ernest Dowson, one line of which reads: "I have forgot much, Cynara! Gone with the wind . . ."

THE ORIGINAL TITLES OF OTHER FAMOUS BOOKS

All's Well That Ends Well = *War and Peace* (by Leo Tolstoy)

The Sea-Cook = *Treasure Island* (by Robert Louis Stevenson)

The Tree and the Blossom = *Peyton Place* (by Grace Metalious)

Fiesta = *The Sun Also Rises* (by Ernest Hemingway)

Something That Happened = *Of Mice and Men* (by John Steinbeck)

The Chronic Argonauts = *The Time Machine* (by H. G. Wells)

Before This Anger = *Roots* (by Alex Haley)

Summer of the Shark = *Jaws* (by Peter Benchley)

GREENLAND ■ The name *Greenland* is a 10th-century example of false advertising. When Erik the Red, a Viking explorer, discovered the ice- and snow-covered island, he gave the place a pleasant, lush-sounding name to attract settlers.

Greenland is the largest island in the world.

GRENADE ■ The small, usually hand-thrown bomb gets its name from the pomegranate, which it resembles in size and shape. (The fruit gets its name from the Latin *pom,* meaning "fruit," and *Granada,* a district of Spain.)

GROOVY ■ The term takes you back to the Hippie Sixties—when such things as long hair, granny glasses, and tie-dyed shirts were groovy.

Actually, the term should take you even further back—to the 1930s. In France at that time, American beatnik musicians wanted to groove, slang for "make a record." The highest compliment that could be paid a musician or a group was to tell them they were groovy—good enough to be recorded.

The term spread to America in the 1950s; by the end of the Sixties, all kinds of things—not just music—were groovy (not to mention far-out, righteous, trippy, and mind-blowing).

GUATEMALA ■ This Central American country got stuck with a lousy name—*Guatemala* means "rotten tree." The name came about because, in some highland areas of the country, there are forests of century plants, so called because of the mistaken belief that they flower only once every 100 years. When they flower, which *is* infrequently, the flower stalk is as large as a man and smells like a corpse!

GUILLOTINE ■ French physician Dr. Joseph-Ignace Guillotin wanted to banish the death penalty. His only reason for inventing the device that bears his name was to make executions faster and less painful, as an interim

The doctor was horrified to see his invention used as a means of mass murder during the French Revolution and for the rest of his life was a tormented man. Until his (natural) death, Guillotin tried desperately—but unsuccessfully—to separate his name from the machine. (The e at the end of the word was added by English poets of the time to ensure that their readers would pronounce the word correctly.)

goal before getting the practice outlawed completely. Dr. Guillotin's original design called for a straight, horizontal blade and did not work well. In a rather horrid bit of irony, he took the plans to King Louis XVI, who helped him design it with an angled blade. The change made it a very effective killing machine—as King Louis would later learn from personal experience: During the French Revolution (1789–1799), he was among those beheaded by the guillotine, and for a time it was called a Louisette.

> The last execution by guillotine took place in Marseilles, France, on September 10, 1977.

GUINNESS® BOOK OF WORLD RECORDS, THE ▪ One day in 1955, Mr. Hugh Beaver came up with the idea for a book that would tell what was the shortest or tallest, fastest or slowest, largest or smallest, etc., in all sorts of categories. On the recommendation of an employee, he contacted twin brothers Norris and Ross McWhirter to compile such a work. Four months later, the first *Guinness Book of World Records,* 198 pages long and bound in green leather, was in bookstores. Where did its name come from? It so happened that Hugh Beaver was the managing director of one of the largest breweries in Ireland—Guinness.

GUN ▪ In the 14th century, Windsor Castle in England was defended by a huge catapult known as Lady Gunhilda—which was shortened to Lady Gun and then just to Gun. In time, the term was applied to any catapult.

> The howitzer, a modern-day cannon that fires its shells with a high trajectory and great range, derives its name from the Dutch word houvietser, meaning "sling."

Invented later in the 14th century in Europe, what we now call guns were at first known as hand cannons. Made of iron, the weapon was about the size and shape of a thick, short length of pipe. As the hand cannons slowly improved, English soldiers began calling them guns.

GUPPY ▪ One day in 1886, R. J. Guppy of Trinidad, a clergyman, was looking into a freshwater pond where a school of tiny, brightly colored fish was swimming. No one seemed to know the name of the fish, so, out of curiosity, he sent live specimens to the British Museum to see if the specialists there could enlighten him. But the scientists at the museum didn't know what the fish were called either. All they

could do was refer to them as the fish sent by Guppy—which soon became their official name.

GUY ■ Today a *guy* is any male person.

It used to be a common first name in England. But then along came Guy Fawkes, the leader of a group of terrorists who tried to blow up the king and the Houses of Parliament one cold November day in 1605. Fawkes was caught in the cellar with thirty-six barrels of gunpowder, taken back upstairs, and hanged.

> In England, November 5 is Guy Fawkes Day, which is celebrated with fireworks and burning effigies (crude likenesses) of Guy Fawkes on a bonfire.

For the next couple of hundred years, Guy was a really unpopular name in England. But at some point, men jokingly began calling one another "guys," and the word stuck.

> If women were caught sneaking a peek at the naked athletes, they were taken to the top of a cliff and pushed off.

GYMNASTICS ■ *Gymnasium* and *gymnastics* take their name from the Greek word *gymnos,* which means "naked." And that's how Greek athletes practiced and competed—in the nude.

GYPSIES ■ During the 15th century in Europe, groups of nomadic people roamed the countryside. They were feared and mistreated, and often called thieves—and worse. Because of their somewhat dark skin, it was believed that they were Egyptians. Shortened at first to *Gyptians,* eventually they came to be known as Gypsies.

HANCOCK, JOHN ■ Not only was John Hancock the first American revolutionary to sign the Declaration of Independence, he wrote his name extra large so that, in his words,

> Hancock hoped to be selected as the commander in chief of the Revolutionary forces and was jealous when General Washington was chosen instead.

"King George [of England] can read my name without spectacles." Today his name is a synonym for the word *signature,* as in "Put your John Hancock on the letter."

HANDBALL ■ Handball originated in Ireland in the 10th century. The early name of the game was fives—in reference to the five fingers on each hand.

HANDICAP ■ The term comes from medieval England, where it referred to a disabled person begging with cap in hand and also to a man taking off his hat as a show of respect and humility. Later, in the 16th century, the words were reversed in naming a type of lottery game called hand in cap. In the game, the winner of one round of the game was penalized—"handicapped"—during the next round to make the odds of winning better for the other players.

HANDKERCHIEF ■ The Romans hung small cloths from their belts. The English, borrowing a French word for *cover,* hung *kerchiefs* from their sleeves. It was the "hang" of those kerchiefs that gave us the pronunciation (and former spelling) of the word—*hang-kerchief.* In the early 18th century in England, the spelling changed to *handkerchief,* because it was held in the hand when used to wipe one's brow, mouth, or nose.

HANUKKAH ■ Hanukkah is celebrated for eight days and nights. In Hebrew, the word means "dedication." The holiday celebrates the rededication of the holy Temple in Jerusalem after the Jews' victory in 165 B.C. over Antiochus, the Greek king of Syria who had outlawed Jewish rituals and ordered the Jews to worship Greek gods.

"HAPPY BIRTHDAY TO YOU" ■ In 1893, Patty and Mildred Hill, schoolteachers from Kentucky, wrote a song entitled "Good Morning to All" as a daily greeting to their classes. To their surprise, in 1924, they found their song published in a songbook with a few new words and a very new name—"Happy Birthday to You."

HARLEM GLOBETROTTERS ■ The team started out in 1927 as the Savoy Big Five. Together with the players, the team's manager, Abe Saperstein, changed the name to the Harlem Globetrotters. "We chose Harlem," said Saperstein, "because Harlem was to our black players what Jerusalem was to [a Jewish person like] me. As for Globetrotters, well, we had dreams. We hoped to travel."

> *The Harlem Globetrotters did not play any games in Harlem for their first forty-one years! 1968 was the first year in which they made an appearance there.*

HEARSE ■ A *hearse* started off as a farming tool. Next it became a type of candleholder. And ended up as a car used to transport dead bodies. Here's how . . .

In France in the 10th century, farmers used a large, triangular rake called a *herse*. Huge and heavy, with long, sharp iron spikes, *herses* were pulled by teams of horses to break up hard soil.

In the 11th century, the English borrowed the word. They used it to describe a large candleholder—one that resembled the oversized, triangle-shaped rake of the past.

Such candleholders were for funerals. A mourner at the head of a procession carried the herse, with its candles burning.

Over time, the spelling changed to the slightly fancier *hearse*. And a hearse itself became more elaborate: By 1600, it was a wooden casket borne along by a horse-drawn cart, leading a procession and decorated with artificial flowers and candles. The hearse also served as a sort of bulletin board on which friends and loved ones pinned poems and notes to the deceased.

By the early 20th century, a hearse had become the term for a large, luxurious car used to carry the dead, as it is today.

HEEBIE-JEEBIES ■ The word first came from the mouth of Barney Google, a cartoon character. The creation of American cartoonist William De Beck (1890–1942), Google sometimes got the jitters, the creeps, or, as he described them, the heebie-jeebies.

HEINZ 57 VARIETIES ■ In 1896, Henry Heinz saw an advertisement for "21 Varieties of Shoes." The sign gave him the idea to advertise his own company's food products with a number. The number *57*, he decided, had a nice sound to it.

He picked it as his company's trademark even though, as he well knew, his company produced more than sixty products. Today, Heinz markets more than fifty-seven *thousand* varieties of food in more than two hundred countries.

(See Ketchup, page 66.)

HELICOPTER ■ The name comes from two Greek words, *helix* ("spiral") and *pteron* ("wing").

The first helicopter to lift a man vertically off the ground was designed by E. R. Mumford of Scotland in 1905. Originally, it was made of bamboo, but when this became waterlogged during a rainstorm, the inventor switched to metal. In 1912, with six huge rotors twirling overhead, the pilot rose ten feet in this air. Because the contraption had no steering mechanism, a large ground crew had to use long ropes to steady it and keep it from fluttering away and crashing.

HELLO ■ Until Thomas Edison suggested using "Hello?" most people answered their phones by saying "Ahoy!" (which had been the idea of the device's inventor, Alexander Graham Bell).

Hershey's® Bar ■ In 1876, when Milton Hershey was only eighteen years old, he opened his own candy shop. The business failed after only six months, but he didn't give up. He kept inventing new types of candy and candy-making machinery. In 1894, in Lancaster, Pennsylvania, Milton Hershey concocted the first "bar of choco-

Hershey's KISSES are called that because the machine that makes them looks as though it's kissing the conveyor belt as it drops each dollop of chocolate.

late," as he called it. Costing 3¢ apiece, Hershey's bars were named after their inventor. Also named after the candy maker is the town of Hershey, Pennsylvania, where the streetlights are in the shape of chocolate "kisses."

HIJACK ■ The term came into use during the 1920s and likely derives from *jacker*, meaning "hold-up man." Another theory as to the word's origins: When holding up a truck to steal its cargo, the thief would walk up to the driver's window, say "Hi, Jack!" and pull out a pistol.

HITLER, ADOLF ■ After Hitler rose to power in Germany in 1933, it became a crime punishable by death to name your horse Adolf (which had long been a common name for horses there). The same fate awaited anyone who called Hitler "Schicklgruber."

Why? And why *that* name?

Anna Schicklgruber, Hitler's grandmother, was unmarried at the time she gave birth to Hitler's father, Alois. Not until Alois was five did she get married—to Johan Heidler. But Heidler refused to accept Alois as his son. People made fun of him and called him "Schicklgruber."

Secretly, at the age of thirteen, Alois was able to get a priest to change his name to Heidler. But the priest misspelled it; instead of *Heidler*, he wrote *Hitler* on the official document.

Alois Hitler married three times. He named the fourth child of his third marriage after a distant relative—Adolf.

HOCKEY ■ Ice hockey has been known throughout its long history as shinny, hurley, and bandy. The sport as we know it today originated in eastern Canada. French Canadians there played it with a *hoquet*—a shepherd's staff. English players named the game after the staff, changing the spelling and pronunciation to *hockey*.

HOCUS-POCUS ■ Originally, in medieval England, a magician was called a hocus-pocus—and so were his tricks.

Why?

Because magic shows would always begin with the same Latin chant: *"Hocus-Pocus, tontus, vade celeriter jubeo!"*

It was almost a challenge. The phrase, roughly translated, meant "I will blind your eyes! Come see this done!"

In England during the reign of King James I of England (1567–1625), one of the best and most popular magicians was a performer with the stage name Hokus Pocus.

As the crowd pressed closer, the magic show turned into a gambling game—one filled with trickery, thievery, and all sorts of hocus-pocus!

HODGEPODGE ■ The original spelling of the word was *hotchpotch* and it was a type of stew. Now it's a term for any jumbled-up mess.

HOLIDAY ■ Originally a holiday was a holy day since until fairly recently, most celebrations were of a religious nature. Around 1850, the two words were combined into *holyday*. Near the turn of the 20th century, the spelling changed to *holiday*.

HOLLYWOOD ■ The original name of the Movie Capital of the World was Paradise Valley. In 1923, Paradise Valley was changed into a luxury housing development called Hollywoodland, and a huge sign (with fifty-foot letters and illuminated by four thousand low-wattage bulbs) was erected on Mt. Lee, a hill overlooking the development. One day during a windstorm, the last four letters of the sign fell over, and it's been *Hollywood* happily ever after.

HOME PLATE ■ In baseball, there's a first, second, and third base—each of which is a sand-filled canvas bag. But there's no "home base." Instead, it's called home *plate*. Why? The reason is that, in the earliest days of baseball, home was actually a heavy *plate* of iron.

HOPSCOTCH ■ In this children's game, a player tosses a stone or other marker into a series of numbered rectangles drawn on the ground and then hops through the spaces to pick up the marker after each toss. The word *scotch* has nothing to do with Scotland; instead, it refers to scratching ("scotching") the boxlike design on the ground with chalk.

HORSE RACING ▪ According to regulations, a racehorse's name can be no longer than eighteen letters. Nevertheless, owners go to great lengths to come up with wacky names for their horses. A few examples: PotatoPants, Spendthrift, Mother's Goose, Which One, Why Not, BigBurp, HurryOff, and Waking Booty.

HORSERADISH ▪ *Harsh radish*—that's what the word for this hot, zesty condiment started out as. In popular speech, the word *harsh* was slurred into *horse,* an animal that isn't related in any meaningful way to radishes.

Hot Wheels® ▪ Elliot Handler was one of the original founders of the Mattel Toy Company, and it was his daughter, Barbie Handler, who inspired the invention of the Barbie doll. One day in 1967, Elliot asked his designers to come up with a fast toy car. And they did. The little vehicle they created could reach a speed of *300* mph downhill. Delighted, and using a then-popular expression for a fast car, Handler exclaimed, "Wow, those are hot wheels!"

(See Barbie® doll, page 10.)

HOTEL ▪ The word began as *hostel*—a common room with many beds for guests. But then, in 1774, a man named David Low redesigned an old mansion in

The first building constructed as a hotel was the seventy-three room City Hotel in New York City, which opened its doors in January 1794. At the time, the total population of New York was just 30 thousand people compared to roughly 20 million today.

London. He and his workers divided all of the upstairs area into private rooms. To differentiate his establishment from a hostel, he called it Low's Grand Hotel.

(See Motel, page 76.)

HOUDINI ▪ Houdini began performing magic when he was teenager, and called himself Eric the Great. (His real name was Ehrich Weiss.) When he was fifteen, he read a book that would change his life: *The Memoirs of Robert-Houdin,* an autobiography of one of

When he was just starting out, Houdini did 20 shows a day at a salary of $12 per week.

the greatest magicians of the day. Fascinated, Ehrich wanted to be just like the famous magician and changed his name to Houdini. In his diary, the young man wrote: "I added the letter *i* which means 'like' to his name, and I became Houdini."

Ehrich's brother Theo was also a magician. Beginning in 1892, the two performed together under the name The Houdini Brothers.

HUMONGOUS ■ It's bigger than *HUGE* and larger than *MONSTROUS*. It's a combination of the two words. *Humongous* first appeared in print in a college newspaper in 1967.

HUNKY-DORY ■ The expression *hunky-dory* means that everything's going just fine.

Robbery. Murder. And the name of a street in Japan. They all figure into the strange story of how *hunky-dory* came to be.

In the early days of America's trade with Japan (1800s), most ships docked in the port of Yokohama. The main street of the city, Huncho-dori Street, was the only thoroughfare that was well policed at night.

Sailors caught in the city after dark, and trying to return to their ship through the twisting alleys and byways, were almost certain to be robbed, beaten, and quite possibly murdered. Men given shore leave soon learned never to wander around Yokohama at night. Only when they stayed on the main street was every-thing all right—or hunky-dory.

> In medieval England, a rainbow was called an Iris.

IRIS ■ In their mythology, the Greeks tell of a lovely goddess named Iris, a messenger who walked down from heaven on rainbows. The iris, a delicate flower of widely varying colors, is named after her. So, too, is the colored part of your eye—the green, gray, hazel, brown, or blue.

> The word iridescent, meaning "to shimmer with all the colors of a rainbow," also comes from the name Iris.

ITALY ■ The whole country is now named after what at first was just its southern part, Italia. The word means "land of oxen," or "oxen-grazing land."

IVORY® SOAP ■ Quite by accident, White Soap became *IVORY SOAP*, the soap that floats.

One day in 1878, a worker at Procter & Gamble's Cincinnati factory forgot to turn off the churning soap vats when he went to lunch. When he returned, he discovered his mistake. But since the extra churning didn't seem to have caused any harm, the batch of soap was shipped out to market.

Customers who happened to buy soap from this batch were surprised to discover that it floated in the bathwater. This floating quality was due to the extra churning, which whipped air into the soap liquid. Orders started coming in for the "new type of White Soap, the kind that floats."

Henry Procter, who was in charge of sales for the company, decided not only to continue making floating soap, but also to give it a new name. One Sunday in church, Mr. Procter listened as the minister read from the scriptures: "All thy garments smell of myrrh [that comes from] *ivory* palaces." In that instant, Procter came up with the name he was looking for: White Soap became IVORY SOAP.

> *"99-44/100 % Pure®: It Floats."* Ivory Soap's famous slogan came into being in 1890 when actual laboratory tests showed this high level of purity.

JACKKNIFE ▪ Where do we get the *jack* in *jackknife?* The maker of the first folding knife was an 18th-century Belgian named Jacques de Liège. *Jacques* is the French equivalent of *James.* But the name was wrongly translated into English as *Jack,* and the item came to be known as a jackknife.

JACKPOT ▪ The term *jackpot* comes from a form of poker in which a player has to have a pair of jacks or better to open (start play) in hopes of winning all the money—the jackpot.

Jacuzzi® ▪ Candido "Roy" Jacuzzi was just a young boy when he and his family emigrated from Italy in the early 1900s. Raised in northern California, he held a variety of odd jobs for the family-owned business, Jacuzzi Bros., which made agricultural pumps. Over the ensuing years, he married, had children, and worked his way up to become president of the company. In 1968, seeking a way to help his son who suffered from rheumatoid arthritis, Roy invented the heated whirlpool bath we know today as a Jacuzzi.

JAGUARS, Jacksonville (NFL) ▪ The football team was named before it existed! In 1989, a company called Touchdown Jacksonville! bid for a team in its city. And it confidently announced the new team would be named the Jaguars if awarded a franchise. It took an incredibly long time—four years—but on November 30, 1993, the Jaguars became who their owner said they'd be.

JAI ALAI ▪ Jai alai is a form of handball played with a basketlike racket fastened to the wrist.

The ball in jai alai is harder than a golf ball and has been clocked at more than 150 mph. This makes movement of the jai alai ball the fastest of any sport.

During the Spanish conquest of Mexico, Hernán Cortés learned of the game, which the Aztecs had played for centuries. He took the rules of play and equipment back to Spain. The

Spanish called the sport *pelota,* meaning "ball." Not until the sport began being played in Cuba, in 1900, did its modern name, *jai alai,* which means "happy celebration," come into being.

JAYWALKING ■ In the late 19th century, *jay* was a term used to describe a country bumpkin. When country folk came to the city, they were unfamiliar with traffic lights, signs, and rules—including the one forbidding crossing midstreet on foot. Because jays were most often the ones to break this law, it came to be known as jaywalking.

JC Penney® ■ James Cash Penney opened his first department store in Wyoming and later established new stores in partnership with men he trained. These stores were first called Golden Rule Stores—later, JC Penneys.

Jell-O® ■ Invented in 1845 by Peter Cooper of New York, the gelatin dessert was a flop for its first fifty-two years, selling just barely enough to keep the business going. Uncolored, flavored only with sugar, it neither looked nor tasted very appetizing. And its name was just as bad: *Cooper's Gelatin Dessert.*

In 1897, a man named P. B. Wait bought the rights—and his wife, May Davis Wait, gave the product its name: Jell-O®.

In 1900, a package of Jell-O cost 10 cents.

Then they added fruit flavors: raspberry, orange, lemon, and strawberry. Despite all these improvements, people still weren't buying; Mr. and Mrs. Wait had to sell the company—for $45 to a neighbor, Francis Woodward.

Things didn't improve for the owner, at least in the beginning. By the end of the first year, Woodward's sales had gotten so slow that the factory was filled to overflowing with unsold crates of Jell-O. Ready to give up, Woodward offered the business to one of his workers for $35. The man turned him down.

In 1902, Woodward took a gamble: He scraped together $336 for a magazine ad—for "Jell-O, America's Most Famous Dessert." Suddenly, his product began to move—and it hasn't stopped yet. At present, more than a million packages of Jell-O are sold every day.

As for the name, it is now an everyday part of our vocabulary—and an accepted word in our dictionaries. Like Kleenex, Band-Aid, and many others, the brand name Jell-O has become a synonym for the product.

JETS, New York (NFL) ■ Organized in 1959, the team was first known as the Titans, a name chosen to directly challenge the NFL Giants across town. During the first few years, the team's record and attendance were far from "titanic." In 1962, when David Werblin bought the team, he said: "We need a new image. So we'll begin with a new name—one not so grandiose." He changed the name to the Jets—leaving the name *Titans* to be picked up by Tennessee's pro football team in 1999.

JIGSAW PUZZLE ■ John Spilsbury, a London mapmaker, made the first jigsaw puzzle in 1763. Spilsbury glued a map of England onto a sheet of wood. When it had dried, he cut it into pieces shaped like the various counties that made up the nation. He sold this and other such "map puzzles" to schoolteachers to use "for the purpose of teaching geography." Until about 1880, jigsaw puzzles remained primarily educational devices.

When they first appeared in 1900, cardboard jigsaw puzzles cost 25¢.

Toward the end of the 1800s, they became "entertainments" and were made from a new material of the time—plywood. By the 1900s, cardboard jigsaw puzzles began to appear; today they are almost the only kind available.

Where does the word *jigsaw* fit into all of this? Back in 1760, Spilsbury cut the pieces of the puzzle with a jigsaw—a type of narrow-bladed saw used for cutting irregular lines. And when he went around to schools selling them, he called the item "educational jigsaw puzzles."

One small problem. Spilsbury actually made his puzzles using something called a marquetry saw, a similar but thinner and finer tool than a jigsaw. If he'd known the right name, "jigsaw" puzzles may well have ended up as "marquetry" puzzles.

> *Charles Lang of Armuchee, Georgia, has put together more than 1,170 jigsaw puzzles. Then, after gluing the pieces of each puzzle together, he attaches them to his walls and ceilings. Now the entire interior of his house is covered with nothing but the results of his puzzling hobby.*

JOHN, ELTON ■ This rock star's real name is Reginald Dwight. He formed his first group, Bluesology, in 1966. He took the name Elton John from the first names of Bluesology members Elton Dean and John Baldry.

JUDO ■ Developed by eighteen-year-old Jigoro Kano in the late 19th century, judo is a refinement of a medieval form of unarmed combat, jujitsu. The word *jujitsu* means "soft art"; *judo* has a similar meaning: "the gentle art." As a technique of self-defense, judo relies on the principles of leverage, so that the strength and weight of the opponent are used against him or her.

> *For many years after its invention it was always referred to as kano judo.*

(See Karate, page 66, and Tae Kwan Do, page 122)

KANGAROO COURT ■ A trial by this name is unfair and unregulated.

The name comes from prisons in the early days of Australia—"the land of the kangaroo." The prisoners had their *own* rules. If an inmate broke any of them, he or she was brought before a judge and jury made up of other prisoners. A verdict of guilty was a foregone conclusion; the punishment was usually harsh and often bizarre.

KARATE ■ The name means "empty hand" in Japanese, suggesting a form of self-defense that does not involve weapons. As early as 400 B.C., Buddhist monks in India used a form of karate to defend themselves against wild animals. During the 6th century A.D., handpicked teenage Korean boys were organized into military units to fight invaders of their homeland. Always, their most important weapons were their hands. Karate developed further on the island of Okinawa during the 1600s. Japanese samurai warriors (who always had two swords) conquered the island and strictly outlawed the owning of any weapons by the native inhabitants. As a result, the Okinawans developed many of the unarmed fighting techniques of modern karate. Though the hand may be empty, a karate "chop" can be lethal.

After the Korean War (1950–1953), many U.S. servicemen returning from the Far East brought with them a new skill—and a new word that, by the late 1950s, had begun entering American dictionaries—*karate.*

(See Judo, page 65, and Tae Kwan Do, page 122.)

Kellogg's Corn Flakes® ■ Dr. John Kellogg, a friend of Sylvester Graham, ate seven graham crackers for breakfast every day. In 1906, he created his own health foods, the first being Granola, followed in 1907 by Corn Flakes. Calling himself the "king of corn flakes," Kellogg soon had a booming cereal business.

(See Breakfast Cereal, page 18.)

KETCHUP ■ The weird thing about ketchup is that it's been around for centuries, but not until pretty recently were there any tomatoes in it!

In the 17th century, the Chinese made a thick sauce of spices and pickled fish called *ke-tsiap.* Its popularity spread to Malaysia, where it was known as *kechap.*

In the early 18th century, British sailors tried the Malaysian sauce, liked it, and returned home with samples of what they mistakenly labeled *ketchup.* Trying to duplicate the gooey relish but having little idea as to its ingredients, English cooks created sauces using such things as mushrooms, walnuts, and cucumbers.

Not until it reached America, sometime around 1790, did tomatoes enter ketchup. With yet another change of spelling, the first-known recipe for "tomata catsup" appeared in a 1792 cookbook.

By the mid-1800s, it had become an everyday condiment on American tables. It was known then, as it is today, as ketchup or catsup. Both spellings are considered correct, though *ketchup* is preferred because of its word history.

Until 1876, ketchup was always homemade and took hours to prepare. Then a German-American chef and businessman entered the picture, offering the first mass-produced bottled ketchup. The man was Henry Heinz.

(See Heinz 57 Varieties, page 55.)

KIDNAPPING ■ After the Norman conquest of England in 1066, food was terribly scarce. People fought over every scrap and even committed murder for a single loaf of bread.

Another way of putting food on the table was kidnapping. But it's not what you think: Children weren't taken away and eaten. In England in the 11th century, the word *kid* meant "a young goat," and it was this that was stolen and consumed. Not until the 1900s did *kid* also come to mean "a human child."

Napping is another word that went through a change of meaning. It now means "dozing, sleeping briefly." But back in the Middle Ages, it was a variation of the word *nabbing,* meaning "to steal." (Thus, back then you might say: "I saw him *napping* my money.")

The modern penalty for the crime of kidnapping is severe; the consequence in certain countries is sometimes death. In the Middle Ages, when the crime involved only the stealing of a goat, the penalty was *always* death.

KINGPIN ■ In an old-fashioned form of bowling, there was a kingpin, one that was taller than the rest and decorated with a crown. The meaning of the word *kingpin* now refers to "the most important and dominant person."

KITE ■ Kites were named in the 16th century after a bird of the hawk family. Kites have a broad wingspan and a long, tapering tail, and can remain in one place in the air for an impressive length of time by heading into the wind.

KIWI® Shoe Polish ■ William Ramsay first marketed the shoe polish in 1906, naming it in honor of his wife. No, her name wasn't Kiwi! And she wasn't a flight-less bird! But she *was* from New Zealand. And *Kiwi* is the nickname for a New Zealander.

Kleenex® and Kotex® ■ During World War I, cotton was in short supply. The Kimberly-Clark Company developed a highly absorbent, paper-based substitute to be used as battlefield dressings and as air filters in gas masks.

After the war, the company had a huge surplus of the cottonlike wadding in its warehouses. Quickly, Kimberly-Clark had to come up with products that could be made from it. One was Kleenex. Called Celluwipes when first marketed in 1924, the name was changed to Kleenex, the word a deliberate misspelling of *clean* plus the affix *ex,* meaning "out," Another product was Kotex, a name derived from the first syllable of *cotton* plus *ex.*

KNUCKLE ■ The word *knuckle* used to mean "knee joint" (not a finger joint). Falling to one's knees in subservience is the origin of the expression to "knuckle under."

LED ZEPPELIN ■ First known as the Yardbirds, the British hard-rock group once played a tape of their music for Keith Moon, drummer for The Who. Unimpressed, Moon joked, "That'll go over like a lead zeppelin!" (the British equivalent of the expression "lead balloon"). Delighted, the Yardbirds changed their name to Led Zeppelin and soon became one of the most famous rock bands of all time.

LEFT WING, RIGHT WING ▪ In politics today, a *left-winger* is a liberal; a *right-winger* is a conservative. These terms, which indicate a politician's general point of view, originated in the French National Assembly during the 1700s. There, all the delegates of the conservative party sat on the right, those of the liberal party on the left.

LIFE SAVERS® ▪ LIFE SAVERS were invented in 1912 by Clarence Crane, a Cleveland chocolate maker who wanted a sweet product that wouldn't melt in the summer heat. Initially, the white circular mints were made on a pharmaceutical pill ma-

When Crane came up with the name and shape of LIFE SAVERS in 1912, life preservers—the round kind with a hole in the middle—were just beginning to be used on ships.

chine and were advertised as "Crane's Peppermint Life Savers—5¢—For That Stormy Breath." The hole in the middle of LIFE SAVERS is patented as "Nothing enclosed by a circle."

The first fruit-flavored variety was the lemon roll of 1924.

LIMOUSINE ▪ It started out as an item of clothing. . . .

In medieval times, the people of the French province of Limousin sometimes wore a visored hood, which came to be known as a *limousin*. In the 18th century, luxurious, horse-drawn carriages were made in the region—ones that had an enclosed area for passengers and a roof (or hood) for the driver. The fancy, hooded carriages became known as *limousines* and years later, so did luxury, chauffeur-driven automobiles.

(See Chauffeur, page 28.)

LISTERINE® ▪ Gross! Back in the early 1800s, not only were operating rooms unsanitary, but the surgeons were too. Doctors would go straight from examining corpses in the morgue to operating on living patients—without even washing their hands!

Englishman Dr. Joseph Lister changed all this, educating doctors about bacteria and pioneering sanitary surgical techniques and conditions.

In 1880, Dr. J. Lambert of St. Louis invented an antibacterial mouthwash—naming it LISTERINE in honor of Dr. Lister.

"LITTLE JACK HORNER" (nursery rhyme) ■

> *Little Jack Horner*
> *Sat in a corner*
> *Eating his Christmas pie.*
> *He stuck in his thumb,*
> *Pulled out a plum,*
> *And said, "Oh, what a good boy am I!"*

Jack Horner was a real person, a steward who worked for a man named Richard Whiting in the 1500s. One day, Whiting entrusted Horner to deliver the deeds to twelve mansions to King Henry VIII of England. The valuable documents were concealed in a pie. On the way, Horner stole the deed to one of the most expensive mansions for himself. The word *plum* in the nursery rhyme is a play on words. It refers not only to the fruit, but also to something that's the best or most valuable.

LITTLE ORPHAN ANNIE ■ Incredibly, the comic strip "Little Orphan Annie" was originally called "Little Orphan Otto." T. H. Gray, its creator, changed the title—and his main character from a boy to a girl—a few months before the strip first appeared.

The ageless little girl with ovals for eyes made her debut in the *New York Daily News* on August 5, 1924. Her dog is named Sandy; her adoptive parents are Mr. and Mrs. Silo.

LLAMA ■ The llama has about the silliest name of any animal. In the 16th century, Spanish explorers were roaming around Peru and spotted the rather weird camel-like creature. In Spanish, they asked the local people what the animal was named. *"Que este llama?"* asked the explorers. The natives scratched their heads and asked: "Huh? Llama? What do you mean by *llama*?" The explorers had their answer, or so they thought: The animal was called a llama.

And that's how the creature ended up with a name that, in Spanish, means "name."

LOBBYIST ■ *Lobbyists* are people who try to get government officials to vote for laws that would be favorable to themselves and their businesses. During the 19th century, President Grant was known to spend his evenings at the Willard Hotel in Washington, D.C., the lobby of which was always filled with people hoping to have a chance to curry favor with him. In time, he began scornfully referring to them as "those darn lobbyists."

LOLLIPOP ■ The lollipop got its name from a slang term in northern England. There, a tongue used to be called a lolly.

LONDON, England ■ Centuries ago, the Irish spoke of a place far to the south that was very *lond,* meaning "wild." In time, the city became known as London.

LYNCH ■ A couple of centuries ago, Captain Charles Lynch of Virginia set himself up as judge, jury (and captain) of a kangaroo court. After hearing brief testimony, he had six men hanged. Writing about him, Edgar Allan Poe coined a new word, *lynching,* a term still used to refer to the killing of an accused person without a lawful trial.

(See Kangaroo Court, page 65.)

M

MADONNA ■ The singer's full name is Madonna Louise Veronica Ciccone. The third of eight children in a large, traditional Italian family, she was named after her mother, who died when Madonna was only six years old.

In high school, Madonna was a cheerleader and straight-A student.

OTHER ROCK AND SOUL STARS' REAL NAMES

Alice Cooper = Vincent Furnier

Baby Face = Kenny Edmonds

Bob Dylan = Robert Zimmerman

Bono = Paul Hewson

Eric Clapton = Eric Patrick Clapp

Freddy Fender = Baldemar Huerta

Ice-T = Tracy Morrow

LL Cool J = James Smith

Pat Benatar = Patricia Andrejewski

Meatloaf = Marvin Aday

Queen Latifah = Dana Owens

Ringo Starr = Richard Starkey

Seal = Henry Samuel

Sid Vicious = John Beverly

MALCOLM X ▪ The birth name of the African-American activist was Malcolm Little. And because of his hair color and the nearness of his home to Detroit, he acquired the nickname "Detroit Red." While in prison, he converted to Islam and changed his name to Malcolm X, the *X* symbolic of one of the many evils of slavery—the destruction of one's identity.

M&M'S® ▪ The two *M*'s stand for the last names of candy makers Forrest Mars and Bruce Murrie. First sold in cardboard tubes, the candy became a favorite of American soldiers during World War II as a quick energy booster.

MARATHON ▪ In 490 B.C., a vastly outnumbered Greek army defeated the Persians on the plains of Marathon. A messenger named Pheidippides ran more than twenty-six miles to Athens to deliver the news and after doing so fell dead from exhaustion. The marathon, a footrace of twenty-six miles, was first staged at the revival of the Olympic Games at Athens, Greece, in 1896.

Marathons are not always races. During the 1920s and 1930s, a marathon dance craze swept the country. The object of these strange contests was to see which couple could dance the longest and win the prize money. With only a few minutes rest every hour, men and women staggered around the dance floor in utter exhaustion for weeks, or even months. (5,148 hours—214¼ days— is the world record.) Spectators paid to see the darkly humorous antics and agony of the dancers. Dancers passed out; some began acting insane; some even died of heart attacks and strokes.

MARIGOLD ■ During one of the early Crusades, Christian soldiers discovered a plant with a striking yellow flower. In honor of the Virgin Mary, they called it Mary's gold. Slurred in common speech, the name of the plant evolved into *marigold*.

MASON-DIXON LINE ■ The Mason-Dixon line marked the boundary between Pennsylvania and Maryland and was regarded as the dividing line between the North and South during the Civil War. It was named after its surveyors, Charles Mason and Jeremiah Dixon.

MATINEE ■ Curiously, our word *matinee*—"an afternoon show"—comes from the French word *matin,* which means "morning." The reason: Originally, in medieval times, such entertainments (often puppet shows) were performed in the morning.

Maxwell House® Coffee ■ In 1874, traveling salesman Joel Creek developed a new coffee blend. One of his customers was the Maxwell House hotel in Kentucky. When the blend became very popular at the hotel's restaurant, Creek decided to name it Maxwell House Coffee.

Years later, Teddy Roosevelt, the twenty-

When coffee was introduced to Europe in the 16th century, it was considered a medicine and could only be purchased with a doctor's prescription.

sixth president of the United States, tasted the coffee. When asked if he would like another cup, Roosevelt answered, "Will I have another? I'd be delighted! It's good to the last drop." Roosevelt's remark—"Good to the last drop"—was quickly picked up as a slogan for Maxwell House Coffee.

MAYONNAISE ■ In the 19th century, a French politician sampled the condiment while in the city of Mahon on the Spanish island of Minorca. Returning to France with the recipe in hand, he called it "sauce of Mahon." French chefs changed the name to mahonnaise. A century later, its spelling again altered, mayonnaise reached America.

McDonald's® ■ One day in 1948, two teenage brothers, Dick and Mac McDonald, chalked

The first hamburger fast-food chain was White Castle, founded in 1916 by J. Walter Anderson of Wichita, Kansas. He sold 5¢ hamburgers along with fries and a cola.

out a design for a new type of restaurant on a tennis court. To attract customers, twin golden arches would be built to form an *M,* their last initial. And they would make their operation more efficient than any other restaurant. They planned to get rid of all unnecessary expenses so that they could sell burgers at the lowest possible price: 15¢. (Fries: 12¢. Malts and shakes: 20¢.) Doing this, they hoped, would increase the number of customers, the greater volume leading to higher profit. Their first McDonald's (in San Bernadino, California) was very tiny—it didn't even have indoor tables. Customers ordered their food at a window and then ate in their cars.

Dick and Mac used the latest, fastest equipment, including the Multimixer, a milkshake machine that could turn out six shakes

Fast food—the restaurant chains as well as the term—did not become popular until the 1960s.

at a time. One day in 1954, Ray Kroc, a Multimixer salesman, visited the restaurant after learning that its owners had bought eight Multimixers (enough to make almost fifty shakes at the same time). Impressed by the operation, Ray suggested to the McDonald brothers that they could make a fortune if they opened several such fast-food restaurants. "Nah, too many headaches," said Dick. "And who could we get to run the places?" asked Mac.

"How about me?" asked Ray.

In 1961, a contract was drawn up entitling the brothers to a percentage and giving Ray Kroc the right to open as many of the restaurants as he wanted. Then, on a scrap of paper, Ray drew a picture of golden arches, which he thought should remain a part of the design and at the same time become the new name of the restaurant chain: Golden Arches Burgers. But Mac and Dick insisted it should remain McDonald's.

MEDITERRANEAN SEA ▪ *Mediterranean* is a Latin word that means "in the middle of the land." The name is an apt one, because the sea lies between northern Africa and southern Europe.

MEXICO ▪ When Cortés conquered the land in 1519, he called the country New Spain. When the people got their independence, they renamed it Mexico, after the ancient word *Mexica,* the Aztecs' name for themselves.

Harry S Truman (U.S. president, 1945–1953) didn't have a middle name. The S isn't an initial; it's just an S.

MIDDLE NAMES ▪ In 1620, when the *Mayflower* sailed for America, nobody aboard had a middle name. The reason: They were illegal. A law of the time stated: "A man cannot have two given names at baptism; on bills of sale that purchaser shall have only a [first and last] name." Basically, the law was meant to keep a person from using two different names to swindle someone during a business transaction.

Donald F. Duck has a middle name. It's Fauntleroy, the name of the main character in Frances Burnett's 1896 children's book entitled Little Lord Fauntleroy.

In the first federal census, in 1790, not one person in the United States had a middle name. Not until the 1800 census did middle names start popping up.

(See Surnames, page 121.)

MOLOTOV COCKTAIL ▪ The people of Finland, while fighting for their independence from Russia during the 1930s, were the first to use Molotov cocktails, gasoline-filled bottles with rag wicks that could be lobbed at buildings and vehicles to set them on fire. The premier of Russia at the time was a man named Molotov.

MONTHS OF THE YEAR ■ The word *month* comes from an Old English word, *mōna,* meaning "moon."

In ancient Greece, public heralds called out the first day of each month. A calend—that what the announcement was called and the term from which we get the word calendar.

The original Roman calendar had ten months. When January and February were added, January 1 replaced March 1 as New Year's Day.

January is named for Janus, the Roman god of beginnings and endings. He had two faces, one looking forward to the future, the other looking backward to the past.

February is named after a Roman festival of purification, the Februa.

March gets its name from the Roman god of war, Mars.

April was originally the second month of the Roman calendar and comes from Latin for "second," aprilis.

May is named for Maia, the Roman goddess of increase.

June is derived from Junius, the name of a Roman family.

July gets its name from Caesar—Julius, that is.

August was named by the Roman senate to honor Augustus Caesar.

September gets its name from the Latin word septem, meaning "seven," since it was the seventh month of the earliest Roman calendar.

October was originally the eighth month—its name is from Latin for "eight," octo.

November, now our eleventh month, comes from Latin for "nine," novem.

December derives from decem, Latin for "ten."

MOSCOW, Russia ■ *Moskva*—in Russian, that's the name of the country's capital. The city's name comes from a Finnish word meaning "waterway." At the intersection of many river trade routes, the town prospered and grew under the rule of Daniel, the grand prince of Moscow (1280–1303).

MOTEL ■ The first motel was the Motel Inn, in San Luis Obispo, California, which opened its doors in December 1925. With a capacity of 150 guests, each room had a private bathroom and telephone and a parking space right outside the door. The designer, Arthur Heinman, coined the word *motel,* a fusion of the words *motor* and *hotel.*

(See Hotel, page 59.)

MOTHER GOOSE ■ Mother Goose was a real person—Elizabeth Vergoose. Her son-in-law, a printer, was annoyed by the rhymes "Mother Goose" sang to his baby. Though he couldn't stand the goofy verses himself, he knew they'd have a lot of appeal to others. He published them in 1719 under the title *Songs for the Nursery; or, Mother Goose's Melodies for Children.*

MOTOWN ■ Why is it called the Motown Record Company? Answer: At first, all the business offices and recording studios were located in Detroit. And because Detroit has long been the center of the American automobile industry, its nickname is Motor Town, or Motown.

MUSHROOM ■ There's no mush in them, and no room either. During the Middle Ages in England, they were called toads' hats. Then, in the 15th century, the English imitated the French word for this fleshy fungus—*mouscheron.* (At the time, the French mistakenly believed mushrooms were a kind of moss: *mousse.*) Garbled into English, *mouscheron* became *mushroom.*

MUSKET ■ A musket was a common bird in medieval France. In the 16th century, the French devised an arrow-firing weapon, which, because it was mostly used for shooting birds, was called a *musket.* When the weapon was adapted for firing bullets, the name was retained.

MYSTERY ■ The word *mystery* comes from the Greek word *mustērion,* "secret rite," which comes from an even older word *muein,* meaning "to shut the eyes."

NAG ■ To *nag* is to annoy a person with persistent scolding, faultfinding, or complaining. Rats. That's what started it. In European cities of the early Middle Ages, rats burrowed under floors, between walls, and up in attics. The constant noise of them gnawing at wood and building nests was enough to drive a person crazy. Germans called the racket *naggen,* from an old Scandinavian term meaning "to gnaw." The English borrowed the term in the 18th century to describe chronic irritation (such as a nagging backache). Eventually, the word evolved to also mean "an annoying person."

NASTURTIUM ■ "Nose twist"—that's what the name of this flower means in Latin. It's an especially fragrant flower, one that would cause a person to twist his or her nose to inhale the sweet, spicy aroma.

NERD ■ A dork, dweeb, loser, geek. A studious social misfit. That's what a *nerd* is.

The word became popular in the United States in the 1950s—frequently popping up in the dialogue of *Happy Days,* a 1970s TV series about the fifties. It was also popular among surfers and drag racers during the period.

> *It may just be coincidence, but Theodor Geisel, better known as Dr. Seuss, first used the word. In If I Ran the Zoo (1950), a Seussian character blabbers, "I'll sail to Katroo/And Bring Back . . . a Nerkle, a Nerd and a Seersucker too!"*
>
> *For Geisel, nerd was a nonsense word—a humorous, made-up term with little or no meaning.*

The earliest origin of the word may be *nert,* a 1940s slang term meaning "nut." U.S. soldiers picked up the word during World War II. By the 1950s, *nerts* had turned into *nerds.*

NEW YORK ■ In 1624, Dutch settlers named the town New Amsterdam. Twenty years later, in 1644, English soldiers conquered it and renamed it New York, in honor of the Duke of York.

The city's nickname is The Big Apple. Why? *Apple* was a slang term for northeastern cities in the 19th century. The largest of these was New York, the *big* apple.

NEWS ■ The contents of the first English-language newspapers were referred to as "currents," "tidings," or "news." "News" came from the Latin *nova*, "things that are new." During the 1800s, many newspaper mastheads pictured a globe with the compass points N, E, W & S, a handy way of saying the articles came from all over the world.

The word nickel means "devil's copper" because the metal is taken from ore containing high levels of arsenic, a poison that killed many miners.

NICKEL ■ Nickels were originally made of silver and called half-dimes. Then, because silver was too costly, it was decided to make the coin out of nickel, a cheaper metal, and a *nickel* it's been ever since.

(See Penny, page 86)

The first Nikes had a rubber sole and nylon top.

Nike® ■ In the early 1960s, Phil Knight, a top runner at the University of Oregon, preferred imported, lightweight European sneakers. After graduating, Knight and his coach, Bill Bowerman, went into the running-shoe business. But Bowerman wanted to take it a step further. Not only should the shoes be lighter, he decided, they should have more traction—grip. One morning he had a sudden inspiration. He plopped a piece of rubber into a waffle iron! By 1962, Bowerman and Knight were making Nikes, cooking up what soon became the standard design for running shoes worldwide. The name itself is that of the Greek goddess Nike, the winged goddess of victory.

In the beginning, an employee of the company (then called Blue Ribbon Sports) sold the shoes out of the back of his van at high school track meets. Today, Nike is the largest sports-and-fitness company in the world.

(See Adidas®, page 4, and Tennis Shoes, page 124.)

NOME, Alaska ■ A British geographer came upon the town around 1850 but was unable to learn its name. He wrote "? Name, Alaska" on his map. His handwriting was so bad that the word was later misread as *Nome*.

NOSTRILS ■ Nostrils were first known as nose thrills. Originally, a *thrill* was a tube or passageway.

Noxzema® ■ This thick white lotion was first sold as Dr. Bunting's Sunburn Remedy until the manufacturer discovered that it "knocks eczema" (severe dry skin) too.

Oh Henry!® ■ This brand of candy bar was named after a boy who used to come into the Williamson Candy Company factory to flirt with the girls who worked there. Every time the girls needed something done, they would call, "Oh, Henry!" and a moment later he'd be hurrying off to do some sort of errand for them.

One day, the owner of the company was trying to think of a name for a new type of candy bar. Nothing came to mind. But then a familiar call rang out: "Oh, Henry!"

OSCAR ■ *The Academy Award of Merit*—that's the official name for an Oscar and what it was called at the first awards banquet in Los Angeles in 1929. Not until the late 1930s did it become known as an Oscar.

The Oscar statuette is a shiny gold knight standing on a reel of film holding a crusader's sword.

At first, Oscars were solid bronze. During World War II, when metal was scarce, plaster was used. Now the statuettes are gold-plated metal.

Has an Oscar ever been refused? Yes, three times.

It received its name, some say, when movie industry librarian Margaret Herrick saw one and laughingly commented, "It looks like my uncle Oscar!" (Oscar Pierce).

That's one version. A second is that actress Bette Davis joked that the backside of the statuette looked like that of her husband, Harmon Oscar Nelson.

Which of these is the correct story? Perhaps both had something to do with how the award got its name. Perhaps neither. In Hollywood, where fact and fiction are always in a tangle, it's impossible to be sure! Regardless, the name for the award officially became Oscar in 1939.

OZ ■ L. Frank Baum loved to reach into his imagination and tell his four sons whimsical stories. Most took place in a fantasy city in which everything was green. During the telling of one such tale, one of the boys asked what this wonderful kingdom was called. Baum looked around the room, and his gaze came to rest on a file cabinet in the corner.

Born with a weak heart, Frank Baum was a sickly, shy child who kept to himself and made up imaginary places and playmates.

When he was only fifteen, Frank started his own newspaper. Called the Rose Lawn Home Journal, it contained articles, stories, and word games. Printed on a small hand-operated press, the newspaper was a success.

Without thinking, he spoke what he read on the lowermost drawer, the one marked *O–Z*.

For several years after the first Oz book was published, it was banned from the shelves of some libraries across the country. Why? Because many librarians felt it did not qualify as important juvenile literature.

PACIFIC OCEAN ■ In the 1600s, Portuguese explorer Ferdinand Magellan had the good fortune to cross the largest and one of the most tumultuous oceans on Earth without encountering a storm, so he called it Mar Pacifico, Portuguese for "calm sea." The Canadian Indians, on the other hand, had a very low opinion of the ocean and called it Stinking Lake.

PACKERS, Green Bay (NFL) ■ In 1919, a young man named Earl "Curly" Lambeau was working for the Indian Packing Company in Green Bay, Wisconsin. During his time off, Curly played football with his buddies as much as he could. One day in August, he asked his bosses at Indian Packing to help him and his friends start up a semipro team. They needed money for equipment and the use of the company's athletic field. After a lot of discussion, the owners agreed.

At first, they were going to call themselves the Indians. But the company changed its name to the Acme Packing Co. Instead of the Green Bay Acmes, decided the players, Green Bay Packers sounded better.

PAGO-PAGO ■ In the 19th century, a time when printers used individual lead letters to print documents, a typesetter ran out of the letter *n*. This port city in Samoa was actually Pango-Pango!

PAKISTAN ■ The country was named fourteen years before it existed!

Although Pakistan did not become a country until 1947, its name was created back in 1933 in anticipation of the eventual creation of the nation. Carved out of the northern part of the Indian Empire, the name is an acronym: *P* is for Punjab; *a* is for Afghanistan; *k* and *i* are for Kashmir; *s* for Sind; and *tan* for Baluchistan.

Coincidentally (and accidentally) *pak* means "holy" and *stan* means "land"; thus, *Pakistan* means "holy land."

PANCAKES ▪ Considered by historians to be "humankind's earliest prepared food," pancakes have gone through an incredible number of name changes. Early Christians called them Shriving cakes because they were served on Shrove Tuesday, the day before the start of Lent. The Narragansett Indians called their version *nokehick* (meaning "soft cake"), which the Pilgrims garbled into no cake. Western pioneers called them hoe cakes because they were frequently cooked over a fire on a garden hoe. At this time, they were also known as ashcakes, or ashpone, since they were often gritty with ashes from being cooked over open campfires. Not until the 19th century did the breakfast food come to be popularly known as pancakes or griddle cakes since pans and griddles had become the preferred utensils for cooking them. Continuing the confusion over the name, they're also known as flapjacks—because they are flat and hang loose like a flap, and jack because they jack up (rise) as they cook.

PANDEMONIUM ▪ Pandemonium is not a pretty sight. In fact, it's hell. It's a scene of wild disorder and noise. John Milton created the word for his epic poem *Paradise Lost* (1667). In the poem, Pandemonium is the capital of hell and means "all demons." Milton made the word by joining the Greek words *pan* (meaning "all") and *daimon* ("demon").

PANTS ▪ Saint Pantaleon is the patron saint of Venice, Italy. In the 15th century, many boys were named after him. By the 16th century, it had become such a common name that one of the characters in a popular comedy of the time was named Pantalone. He played the role of a fool who wore silly-looking trousers—they were tight from the ankle to the knee, and then flared out like a petticoat. In France, they were called *des pantalons;* in England, pantaloons. Again and again, the style changed. For a time, the

In England, pants means "underwear."

garment looked like a pair of tights, and was often worn with a skirt. This evolved into knee breeches—the short trousers worn with knee-high socks of the 17th and 18th centuries. In America, English colonists gradually lengthened their pantaloons—and shortened the name to pants. Not until the 19th century did the word appear in print—in a short story by Edgar Allan Poe.

PARIS, France ■ In ancient times, warriors of the Parisii tribe settled on an island in the River Seine. In time, this became the center of the city that would eventually grow up around it on both banks of the river.

Conquered by the Romans in 52 B.C., its name became Lutetia. But gradually it came to be known as Parisii, bringing back the name of the original inhabitants. The ruling Romans liked the name but shortened it to Paris, which was the name of a handsome young man of Greek legend. According to the legend, the bloody Trojan War began when Paris kidnapped Helen, the beautiful wife of a Greek king.

PATRIOTS, New England (NFL) ■ The team began in 1959 as the Boston Patriots, then changed its name to the New England Partiots, becoming the first and only pro football team named after a general region of the country rather than a city or state. The nickname Patriots, selected by a panel of Boston sportswriters, suggests the fact that Boston and New England were the birthplace of the American Revolution—and many of the country's patriots.

PAUL REVERE'S MIDNIGHT RIDE ■ In 1861, Henry Wadsworth Longfellow wrote a poem entitled *Paul Revere's Ride*. According to this famous poem, Revere, during the outbreak of the American Revolution, rode alone to warn the colonists: "The Redcoats [British soldiers] are coming!"

> *Listen, my children, and you shall hear*
> *Of the midnight ride of Paul Revere.*

Actually, *two* men made the historic ride, Paul Revere and William Dawes. Not only that, but it was Dawes who rode first, rode longest, and did the whole job right. Revere, meanwhile, got sidetracked and was captured by British troops.

So, why isn't the poem called *The Midnight Ride of Dawes and Revere,* immortalizing both men? It's likely that Longfellow simply had his facts wrong. His poem was written eighty-five years after the famous ride, and details of the event had been obscured by time. Dawes was a little-known shoemaker. Revere, on the other hand, was a prosperous and well-known silversmith. Longfellow undoubtedly had seen silverware made by Revere and been told of the man's daring deed—but it's quite unlikely that the poet had ever seen a pair of shoes made by Dawes.

Paul Revere took his midnight ride on a horse named Brown Beauty. No one seems to remember the name of William Dawes's horse.

PEANUTS ■ Throughout their history, peanuts have had all sorts of names: groundnuts, ground peas, goobers, earth nuts, and monkey nuts. The Planters Company, the first to try to sell the food as a snack, is responsible for standardizing the name. In 1916, to create a distinctive trademark, the company sponsored a drawing contest. The winner was a fourteen-year-old boy who drew a crayon picture he titled "Little Peanut Person." The boy won $5. An artist hired by the company added a cane, top hat, and monocle and called the character Mr. Peanut—the name by which he's been known ever since.

Kind of crazy, but a peanut is not a nut at all. It's a type of seed.

PEANUTS Comic Strip ■ Charles Schulz's famous cartoon strip was originally called "Li'l Folks." Most people think its main character was named after the cartoonist himself. Actually, the clumsy hero is named after one of Schulz's best friends, Charlie Brown. Snoopy was originally going to be named Sniffy, until Schulz discovered that the name was already being used in another comic strip.

Extremely shy, Charles Schulz never once asked a girl on a date—he was too afraid of being turned down. In his senior year of high school, he mustered the courage to submit some of his cartoons to the editors of his class yearbook. His work was rejected.

Today, "Peanuts" is the most widely read comic strip in the world, and one of the most famous.

PEARL JAM ■ The alternative rock group originally called itself Mookie Blalock in honor of a player for the Atlanta Braves baseball team. The name of the band's first album was *Ten,* Mookie's jersey number. Just before the release of *Ten,* the group decided to change the band's name. Eddie Vedder, the lead singer, came up with Pearl's Jam, after his grandmother Pearl and the great jam she made. Besides, *jam* was a nice play on words, suggesting a musical jam session. Other band members liked the name; but after talking about it for a while, they decided to simplify the name to Pearl Jam.

PEEPING TOM ■ In English legend, Lady Godiva was an 11th-century beauty who rode naked down the main street of the town of Coventry, England, on a white horse. Why? Her husband, the mayor, had levied extremely high taxes on the townspeople. Lady Godiva begged him to lower them. He refused. She kept begging. Eventually, more to make her quiet than anything else, he said he would cut taxes if she agreed to ride unclad through town.

To her husband's astonishment, Lady Godiva accepted the challenge. Legend has

Godiva chocolates are named after the brave lady.

it that before going on her daring ride, she asked all the townspeople to stay indoors and keep their shutters closed. All did except for a tailor named Tom, who peeped out a window.

PENITENTIARY ■ A *penitentiary* was originally a room in a church. It was the place for penitents, people who had committed a sin and needed to be alone to think about what they had done and to pray for forgiveness. Today, the word means "a large prison, usually one for hardened criminals serving long sentences."

PENNY ■ It may sound totally crazy, but the penny was originally called a nickel—since it was made of this metal.

When the penny was first minted (in 1785), Congress stipulated that "200 shall pass for one dollar." Two months later, this was changed so that 100 pennies equaled a dollar.

Later, when it was made of copper, people started calling it a penny after the British pence, a copper coin of similar value.

(See Nickel, page 79.)

Pepsi-Cola® ■ Created in 1897, it was first called Brad's Drink. Why? Because its inventor was Caleb Bradham, a young pharmacist from North Carolina. In 1902, Bradham changed the name to Pepsi-Cola because of the pepsin and kola nuts used in the recipe.

In 1963, the company used the slogan "Come Alive—You're in the Pepsi Generation." Consumers in China found this a bit confusing. In Chinese, it roughly translates as "Pepsi Brings Your Ancestors Back from the Dead."

PERFUME ■ Perfume was invented to mask the odor of burning flesh. In the Middle East in ancient times, it was common to sacrifice animals to the gods. To cover the stench of burning carcasses, sweet-smelling resins such as frankincense and myrrh were thrown on the fire. The word is a compound of *per* and *fumus,* Latin for "through the smoke."

PERM ■ The perm—short for *permanent wave*—was invented in Germany by Karl Nessler in 1906. After a thick paste of borax had been applied, the woman's hair was then wound around twelve curlers, each of which weighed two pounds! And then she sat—for six hours!—waiting for her hair to get curly.

PEZ® ■ They started out as an aid to quit smoking. In 1927, Eduard Haas of Austria created a new peppermint candy, an adult breath mint and alternative to cigarettes. He called it PEZ; short and easy to remember, the name comes from the first, middle, and last letters of the German word for peppermint, *Pfefferminz.*

For its first twenty-one years, PEZ candies were carried around in pocket-sized tins. In 1948, the company came out with what they called the "Easy, Hygienic Dispenser." Continuing their substitute-for-smoking idea, the dispensers were shaped like cigarette lighters and worked in much the same manner.

In 1952, PEZ first targeted the American market. But American kids weren't interested. The breath mints were too strong. Quickly understanding the problem,

Haas changed the formula to fruit flavors, each with an appropriate color. And then to make the candies even more appealing to kids, he had dispensers created with humorous plastic heads.

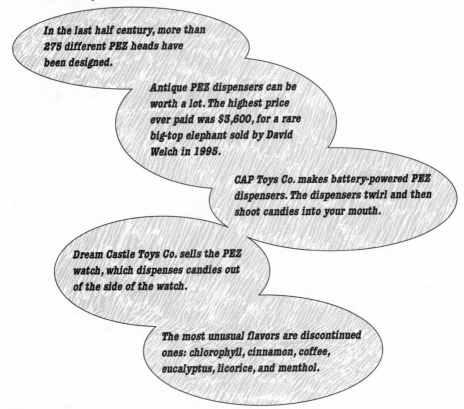

In the last half century, more than 275 different PEZ heads have been designed.

Antique PEZ dispensers can be worth a lot. The highest price ever paid was $3,600, for a rare big-top elephant sold by David Welch in 1995.

CAP Toys Co. makes battery-powered PEZ dispensers. The dispensers twirl and then shoot candies into your mouth.

Dream Castle Toys Co. sells the PEZ watch, which dispenses candies out of the side of the watch.

The most unusual flavors are discontinued ones: chlorophyll, cinnamon, coffee, eucalyptus, licorice, and menthol.

PHONY ■ One trick used by Irish con men in the 19th century involved selling expensive-looking but almost worthless rings called fawneys. And now all kinds of things are "phony."

PICASSO, PABLO ■ The famous Spanish painter and sculptor was the son of painter Jose Ruiz and Maria Picasso. Pablo Ruiz—that was the boy's name at birth. At the age of nineteen, he chose to go by his mother's last name—Picasso—partly because he was closer to her, partly because the name was less common than Ruiz.

PIGGY BANK ■ In medieval Europe, pottery was made of thick, orange-hued clay called *pygg*. Extra coins were saved in *pygg* jars. By the 18th century, the *pygg* jar had become a pig jar, or pig bank. Either not knowing or not caring that the original word had referred to a type of clay, not an animal, potters began making coin banks in the shape of a pig. Soon it became popular to give a child a *pyggy* bank as a gift, which taught the value of saving one's money.

Ping-Pong® ■ In the early 1900s, many sporting goods companies had their own brand names for table tennis. Gossima was the oldest name (coined by James Gibb, who popularized the use of the celluloid ball). Other names were whiff-whaff, house tennis, and flim flam. One day in 1920, an employee of Parker Brothers noticed that the ball made the sound *pong* when it hit the table and *ping* when hit by the paddle. Pong-Ping—that's what it was originally going to be called, until the company decided Ping-Pong sounded better.

PINK FLOYD ■ The original name of the English rock group was Sigma 6. Then they toyed with such names as The Meggadeaths, The T-Set, and the The Screaming Abdabs.

Syd Barrett, the inspiration and founder of the group, went insane from using LSD and other hallucinogens.

In 1965, guitarist Syd Barrett (an original member) named the group The Pink Floyd Sound. American blues artists "Pink" Anderson and Floyd Council inspired the name, soon shortened to Pink Floyd.

PIRATES, Pittsburgh (baseball) ■ The Pittsburgh Pirates got their name as a result of a stunt they pulled in 1880. In that year, the team allegedly stole an important player, Louis Bierbauer, away from the Philadelphia Athletics, offering nothing in return. Newspapers called the Pittsburgh team "a bunch of pirates." The team didn't mind being called that at all. In fact, in 1889, they adopted it as their official name. It was, they decided, a lot better than their old one—the Alleghenies.

PITCHER ■ Originally, a *pitcher* was a leather jug treated with tar pitch to keep it from leaking and to help it keep its shape. Thus, you pour liquid from a container that gets its name from a type of tar.

The baseball player who throws balls and strikes gets his name from *picher*. In the Middle Ages, a *picker* was "one who threw."

PLACEBO ■ In the 13th century, English priests chanted a verse for the dead that began: *"Placebo domino in regione vivorum."* Since the chant, popularly known as "The Placebo," was sung for the dead only to please the living, its usage came to be regarded as a rather empty, self-serving gesture. Centuries later, doctors found that useless sugar pills were sometimes effective in treating patients, especially those with phantom ailments that were "just in their heads." Doctors called such pills placebos, bringing back into popular use the name of the worthless chant.

PLANET NAMES ■ EARTH • The name comes from the early English word *eorthe,* meaning "the ground."

> *Earth is the only planet with oceans of liquid water.*

> *A day on Jupiter is about ten hours long.*

JUPITER • He started out big, as the ruler of all the other Roman gods, so the largest of the planets is named after him. (The last part of Jupiter's name comes from *pater,* meaning "father"; fittingly, the planet has many little moons orbiting around it.)

MARS • was the Roman god of war. Why the nickname Red Planet? Because red is the traditional color of battle and because, even to the naked eye, the planet appears red due to the great amount of iron in its soil. Basically, Mars is rusty!

> *Astrologers of the Middle Ages used the position of Mars in the sky to predict the future.*

> *Mercury has the biggest temperature range of all the planets—from -297°F at night to 845°F during the day!*

MERCURY • With winged sandals on his feet, Mercury was the messenger boy, the speedy errand runner for the other Roman gods. Mercury, one of the smallest planets, speeds around the sun every 88 days. (Earth's orbit, by comparison, takes 365 days.)

NEPTUNE • The Roman god of the sea. The planet was given its name because its surface is wracked by powerful winds, vortices, and storms.

> *This planet has a huge orbit. Since its discovery in 1846, Neptune has not yet completed even one revolution of the sun.*

PLUTO • In Greek mythology, Hades was the god of the under-world. The Romans called him Pluto. Why? Because he was in charge of hell, which was believed to be the region from which wealth came, he took on the name Pluto. This is the masculine form of Plutus, who was the goddess of wealth.

Pluto is smaller than our moon.

The smallest and farthest planet from the sun, Pluto rotates in the opposite direction from the other planets, and its orbit around the sun is tilted compared to the other planets. Because of its small size and erratic orbit, many astronomers believe it should be classified as a large asteroid rather than a planet.

When discovered in 1930, it was called Planet X. Venetia Burney, an eleven-year-old English girl, suggested the name Pluto.

The material of which Saturn is made is less dense than water. A chunk of it dropped in a tank of water would float.

SATURN • The planet with the rings around it is named after the Roman god of the harvest. Galileo was the first to ob-serve it through a tele-scope in 1610.

Saturn has twenty moons—and astronomers keep finding more!

URANUS • In Greek mythology, Uranus was the Greek god of the sky. (And his wife, Gaea, was the earth.)

Astronomer Sir William Herschel spotted the planet in 1781 and named it Georgium Sidus (the "Georgian Planet"), in honor of King George III of England. But people called the planet Herschel after its discoverer. Finally, astronomers de-cided to name it after a mythological figure, to match the names of all the other planets. By 1850 the name *Uranus* had come into popular usage.

VENUS • The brightest planet visible from Earth is named after the Roman goddess of love and beauty. The only planet named after a goddess, its surface features (with few exceptions) are also named for

A year on Venus is shorter than its day! Why? Venus travels around the sun more quickly than it rotates on its axis.

The early Greeks thought Venus was two stars rather than one planet. They called it the Morning Star and the Evening Star.

female figures. For example, Guinevere, Atalanta, and Lavinia are the names given to three wide valleys on the planet's surface.

(See Days of the Week, page 36.)

POINSETTIA ■ American diplomat Joel R. Poinsett of Charleston, South Carolina, became the first U. S. minister to Mexico in the early 19th century. While there, he found a flower the people called flower of the blessed night *(flor de la noche santo)* and brought samples back to the United States. In his honor, the plant with bright red leaves is now called a poinsettia and is a favorite at Christmastime in the United States as well as Mexico.

POODLE ■ Known to be strong swimmers, in Germany they were called *Pudelhunds,* which means "water-splash hounds."

PRINCE ■ The rock star's name is Prince Roger Nelson. He was named for the Prince Roger Trio, led by his father. In 1993, Prince suddenly became "the Artist Formerly Known As Prince" when he changed his name to a symbol that combined the male and female signs: ♀. The unpronounceable symbol was not just to establish a new identity, but also to free him from "undesirable relationships" with record companies. On December 31, 1999, he changed his name back to Prince.

PRIVATE EYE ■ In 1925, the Pinkerton Detective Agency launched a highly successful billboard campaign. It featured a huge picture of an eye and a slogan reading "We never sleep." A detective for hire has been known as a private eye ever since.

In 1861 Allan Pinkerton, founder of the detective agency, uncovered a plot to assassinate President Lincoln (four years before his actual assassination by John Wilkes Booth in 1865). At Lincoln's request, Pinkerton launched the Secret Service, a group of elite agents whose primary task is to protect the president of the United States at "any cost."

Buried near Pinkerton is Kate Warn, who, in 1856, became the first woman detective in the United States.

PULITZER PRIZE ■ Joseph Pulitzer (1847–1911) was a Hungarian immigrant who fought for the Union Army in the Civil War, then went on to become a newspaper publisher in St. Louis and New York City. His will established what are today the most important awards for outstanding work in literature, journalism, and music.

PUMPERNICKEL BREAD ■ As the story goes, Napoléon, the French emperor, sampled this dark brown German bread. Disgusted by the taste, he supposedly exclaimed, "This is bread for my horse Nicole!" The comment in French, *Pain pour Nicole,* sounded a lot to English speakers like *pumpernickel.*

Another version of the word's history has it that *pumpernickel* is a combination of the German words *pumpern,* meaning "to pass gas," and *nickel,* a type of goblin.

PUPIL ■ Why is the dark part of the eye known as the pupil? If you look into a person's eyes, your own miniaturized image is reflected in the pupil's blackness. For this reason, the word *pupil* comes from a Latin word meaning "little doll."

Pupils—as in students—aren't called that because they're little dolls. The name came about because, until recent times, only boys were given an education. The word pupil comes from pupus, Latin for "boy."

From their earliest days, they were known as Quakers because they were said to quake (tremble) in the presence of God.

Many members of the Society of Friends (the official name of the Quakers) were offended by the trademark. Soon after Quaker Oats began appearing in markets, they petitioned Congress to bar companies from using trademarks in any way connected to their religion, but they were unsuccessful.

Quaker Oats® ■ One day in 1887, Henry Seymour was trying to think of a good name for his new oatmeal milling company. He looked through a dictionary, but nothing sounded right. Seymour opened an encyclopedia at random, sat down, and found himself reading an article about Quakers. He was struck by the similarity of the religious group's qualities and the desirable attributes of oatmeal—purity, cleanliness, and wholesomeness. Closing the encyclopedia, Seymour had the name he'd been looking for: Quaker Oats.

QUEEN MARY ■ The famous ship got its name as the result of a misunderstanding.

A representative of Cunard Lines, the company that built the ship, visited King George V of Great Britain and told him the company wanted "to name the ship after the greatest Queen that ever lived." King George assumed the man meant his wife, Queen Mary; instead, he was referring to Queen Victoria (the king's grandmother). Too embarrassed by the misunderstanding to do otherwise, Cunard named the liner after the not-so-great Queen Mary.

RAINCOAT ■ *Aquatic Gambroon Cloak*—that was the clunky name of the first raincoat. In 1747, French engineer François Fresneau created the garment when he waterproofed an old overcoat by smearing it with liquid latex.

Although seventeen-year-old James Syme (who later became a famous surgeon), actually invented effective waterproof fabric, he never bothered to take out a patent on it. He left that to Charles Macintosh, who, in 1830, came out with the first marketable raincoat—a macintosh.

RAMADAN ■ In Arabic, the word *ramadan* means "the hot month" (or, "the scorcher") and derives from *ramada,* "to be hot." The ninth and most holy month of the Moslem calendar, Ramadan is a time of fasting and prayer for those of the Islamic faith.

> *It was during the month of Ramadan that the Koran, "the word of God," was revealed to the prophet Mohammed.*

RAMS, St. Louis (NFL) ■ In 1937, the Cleveland Rams became an NFL franchise. Nine years later, in 1946, they went west and became the Los Angeles Rams. In 1995, they headed back east and became the St. Louis Rams. How did they get the name *Rams*?

Soon after their owner, Homer Marshman, was awarded the franchise in 1937, he met with reporters in Cleveland. He still didn't have a name for the team, he admitted, and asked the newspeople for their suggestions. All agreed the name should not only be tough sounding, but also short—so it would fit easily into a

> *The first NFL team in St. Louis was the Gunners. In 1934, the St. Louis Gunners joined the NFL by purchasing the franchise of the bankrupt Cincinnati Reds NFL team.*

headline. One of the reporters suggested *Rams,* the nickname of Fordham University in New York, a big football school at the time. The name fit both criteria perfectly.

RAP ■ Back in the 1960s, hippies rapped—just "got down" and talked about deep, trippy things. To rap, then, meant to converse freely and candidly.

By the late 1970s, rapping started turning into music—into songs that are rapidly spoken rather than sung.

As for the word itself, *rap* most likely comes from the word *rapport,* which means to have a relationship in which there is communication, agreement, and understanding.

RAVENS, Baltimore (NFL) ■ Edgar Allan Poe, a former Baltimore resident, and his famous poem "The Raven," inspired the name for Baltimore's team. At first, *Ravens* was among a list of one hundred acceptable names prepared by the NFL. A telephone survey of one thousand fans shortened the list to Ravens, Marauders, and Americans. Fans were then asked to participate in a phone-in poll conducted by a Baltimore newspaper. *Ravens* was picked by nearly two-thirds of the fans. Said the owner: "It gives us a strong nickname that is not common to teams at any level, and that means something historically to this community."

Poe was paid $12 for his poem "The Raven" when it was first published in 1845.

Orphaned at the age of twelve, Poe spent only part of his life in Baltimore. He was born in 1809 in Richmond, Virginia—and died there of the effects of drug and alcohol addiction in 1849 at the age of forty.

RED TAPE ■ The term *red tape* refers to exasperating delays caused by seemingly endless government rules and regulations. In England until the 1600s, official government documents were always rolled into a scroll and tied with red ribbon. The English word for ribbon at the time was *tape.*

Sir Walter Scott, author of *Last of the Mohicans* and other works, refers in one of his books to someone "drawing from his pocket a budget of papers, and untying the red tape."

REDSKINS, Washington (NFL) ■ The football team started out in 1932 as the Boston Braves (same as the baseball team). They moved after one year and became the Washington Redskins.

R.E.M. ■ The rock group takes its name from a scientific term. The initials R.E.M. stand for rapid eye movement. When you go into a dream phase during sleep, your eyes move rapidly—back and forth and up and down—beneath closed lids,

as though you were watching a movie. The movement is especially fast and intense during nightmares.

REVLON® ■ Charles Revson was one of the founders of the cosmetics company in 1932. His partner's name was Lachman. In creating a company name, they decided to substitute the initial *l* for the letter *s* in Revson.

RIO DE JANEIRO ■ In 1501, mapmaker Amerigo Vespucci (after whom America is named), was sailing off the coast of Brazil when he spotted a bay he mistook for a river. Since the day was January 1, he called it River of January, or in Italian, *Rio de Janeiro.*

RIPLEY'S BELIEVE IT OR NOT!® ■ In 1909, teenager Robert Ripley got a job as a sports artist. One day in 1918, while working for the *New York Globe,* he was at a loss for an idea to fill his allotted space in the newspaper. In desperation, he looked up a few unusual items about sports. One was about the winner of something called a backwards-walking race. He drew a picture of the thing and captioned it. People liked the feature so much that Ripley's boss asked him to create it on a weekly basis. Ripley eagerly agreed—and soon was producing what he called *"CHAMPS & CHUMPS."*

Doing the strip and finding the facts for it became too time-consuming for one person. Ripley hired Norbert Pearlroth to dig up the weird facts and anecdotes and write them down. Pearlroth suggested that they broaden the scope of the strip to include just about every possible subject area, and in 1919 the name was changed to "Ripley's Believe It or Not!"

Ripley was the one who drew the pictures (a majority of them). But Pearlroth dug up almost all of the facts. For more than fifty years (1923–1975), Pearlroth, who could read eleven languages, pored through thousands of books and ancient manuscripts, always in search of interesting and unusual facts. Rarely taking a day off, he always went to the New York Public Library and sat in the same spot. On the street, he was a nobody, just a guy who wore soft plaid shirts and a wide tie. But once inside that cathedral of books, he was a celebrity (especially to the librarians), a man with an almost endless knowledge of the unusual twists and turns of life.

Robert Ripley eventually had a staff of artists working for him. Pearlroth worked alone, and by himself amassed an incredible amount of material—all of which he could document and prove to be factual. Norbert Pearlroth—at least half of the credit should go to him for "Ripley's Believe It or Not!"

ROBOT ◼ In 1920, Czech writer Karel Čapek was writing a play about mechanical workers who take over the world. The author, wondering what to call the things, decided on *labori.* Čapek's brother Josef didn't think much of the name and insisted it be changed to *robot,* which he derived from the Czechoslovakian words *robotnik,* meaning "peasant," and *robota,* meaning "drudgery" or "dull, repetitive tasks."

How did the word get into English? Entitled *R.U.R.* (Rossum's Universal Robots), Čapek's freaky play was a big hit, especially in London, where it opened in 1921.

> The first functional robot appeared at the 1939 World's Fair. Named Elektro the Mechanical Man, the 7-foot, 260-pound robot (and his robot dog Sparko) was set in motion by the vibrations of the human voice. Electro had a vocabulary of seventy-seven words and could walk forward and backward, count on his fingers up to ten, tell the color of an object held in front of him, and perform several other tricks. A pre-microchip creation by Westinghouse, Elektro's electrical system contained 24,000 miles of wire—enough to circle the globe.

RUGBY ◼ In early English football, players could only kick the ball, not run with it. This all changed one day in 1923, during a game at the Rugby School for boys in Warwickshire, England, when a boy named William Ellis broke the rules by scooping up the ball and running with it. Though Ellis was sent to the bench for this breach of the rules, his actions captured the imagination of other players. Soon a new type of game came into being—one in which the ball could be carried by the runner. The sport was called *Rugby,* after the school where it had its accidental start.

SABOTAGE ▪ Sabotage gets its name from a type of shoe.

Sabot is a French word for wooden shoes worn by the peasants of Europe from 1 A.D. until the beginning of the 20th century. Often they were used like our rain boots of today—as overshoes.

During the 18th and 19th centuries, there were many—often violent—labor disputes between workers and their employers. French factory workers—in protest of low wages, long hours, and generally poor treatment—tossed their sabots into the machinery. This "sabotage," as it came to be known, sometimes destroyed the equipment and almost always delayed production.

The first documented use of the word in English was in a handwritten letter dated 1910 by an English army officer. During World War I (1914–1918), *sabotage* acquired its popular meaning: "the wartime destruction of enemy bridges, railroads, and other military targets, usually by small groups on covert missions."

SAINT BERNARD ▪ This breed of dog is credited with saving thousands of skiers and travelers in snowbound regions. It was named after a Christian monk known as Saint Bernard, who established many monasteries and other shelters for travelers in the Alps during the 12th century. Most of the places kept a breed of big, fluffy, brown-and-white dogs, which became known as Saint Bernard's dogs. In addition to aiding in searches for those who were lost, they were guard dogs and constant companions to the monks. A cook at one of the monasteries had a special job for the Saint Bernards. He built an exercise wheel to which a dog could be harnessed. When the dog walked, a cooking spit would turn!

SAINTS, New Orleans (NFL) ▪ Pro football's Saints got their name from a song—the classic New Orleans jazz tune "When the Saints Come Marching In." Fittingly, the expansion team was officially awarded an NFL franchise on November 1, 1966—All Saints Day.

The Saints first took the field the following year, 1967.

SALISBURY STEAK ■ In 19th-century England, Dr. James Henry Salisbury advocated shredding or otherwise tenderizing all food before eating it (to make it easier to digest). Salisbury also proclaimed the health benefits of eating beef three times a day—and washing it down with warm water.

Doc Salisbury had a large following, and "Salisbury vegetables" and "Salisbury fruits" were included in the daily fare of his converts. Only Salisbury steak has survived the test of time.

SARCOPHAGUS ■ A *sarcophagus* is a coffin made of stone. Often it is beautifully and intricately carved. Usually, it is aboveground.

These first stone coffins were made from a special type of limestone that supposedly had the power to eat flesh! That is why *sarcophagus* comes from the Greek words *sarkos* (flesh) plus *phagein* (to eat). The name literally means "flesh eating."

Flesh-eating stone is not just superstition or silly folklore: This type of limestone does actually cause rapid disintegration of the contents. Flesh and fluids are absorbed into the cavities of the porous stone.

SAXOPHONE ■ Antoine Sax (1814–1894) grew up with his ten brothers and sisters in Brussels, Belgium. As a child, he loved working at the side of his father, a maker of wind instruments. While trying to improve the tone of a bass clarinet, Antoine ended up inventing a brand-new instrument. Blowing his own horn, he named it the Saxophone.

Schick® Electric Razor ■ The name comes from a retired American colonel, Jacob Schick, an Iowan who invented the electric razor in 1931. In German, *Schick* means "elegance." But his first models didn't live up to their name: Far from elegant (or even much good), they consisted of a large motor in a box with a flexible electric line connected to the handheld shaver.

Before Jacob Schick manufactured the first electric razor in 1931, there was Samuel Bligh's Beard Grinder of 1900.

When he was only sixteen, Jacob Schick was in charge of a railway line that ran from Los Corrillos, New Mexico, to a coal mine owned by his father.

Powered by a sewing machine, the contraption consisted of a sandpaper-like roller against which the man would put his face and chin. (Which may explain why so many men chose to have beards back then!)

Schick became obsessed with shaving and believed that a man could extend his life to 120 years by correct, everyday shaving.

SCOTLAND YARD ■ At present, Scotland Yard is the headquarters of the London police. During the 10th century, the plot of ground was given to the king of Scotland to erect a residence for his visits to England.

SCUBA ■ The word is an acronym for self-contained underwater breathing apparatus. The equipment worn by scuba divers consists of one or two compressed-air tanks strapped to the back and connected by a hose to a mouthpiece.

Alexander the Great (336–323 B.C.), in addition to conquering much of the ancient world, also made the first scubalike dive—the first attempt at underwater exploration in an apparatus containing air. He had a huge, transparent glass bell made. When lowered into the sea, it formed a natural air pocket in which the diver could breathe and look around.

SENATOR and SENATE ■ Deriving from Latin, *senator* means "old man"; *senate,* "a group of old men."

The Roman senate was an all-male thing. No women allowed. It was the same way in the United States until 1932. On January 12 of that year, Hattie Ophelia Caraway, a Democrat from Arizona, became the first women elected to the Senate. Reelected twice, she served until 1945.

7 UP® ■ In 1920, in the small town of Price's Branch, Missouri, Mr. C. L. Griggs invented a popular orange drink called Howdy. His next idea for a beverage was something he called Bib-Label Lithiated Lemon-Lime Soda. People liked the taste but not the long, clumsy name. For weeks, Griggs tried to think of something a little less goofy sounding. Then one day while on an errand, he passed a bankrupt chocolate-bar company, 7-Up. It was the perfect name for his product, he decided.

The *7* would stand for the seven-ounce bottle used for the beverage, and the word *UP* suggested "bottoms up," a phrase commonly used before taking a drink.

SHAMBLES ■ Today a *shambles* is a mess, with everything thrown every which way—such as, "Your room is in a shambles."

Originally, the word referred to a *bloody* mess. Back in the 18th century and 19th centuries, a *shambles* was a butcher shop or slaughterhouse—with animal carcasses and cuts of meat all over the place.

SHAMPOO ■ In India during the 1800s, the word *champo* meant "massage the scalp" and referred only to this part of having one's hair washed. British soldiers based in India thought the word referred to the soap and to the entire hair-cleaning process. By the early 1900s, liquid soap had been invented. Mixing it with oils and sweet scents, the English used it to wash their hair. Retrieving a word from their past, they called it shampoo.

Shell Oil Company® ■ In the early 1800s, Marcus Samuel owned a little curio shop in London. Upon returning from a vacation, Mr. Samuel's children glued seashells to their lunch boxes. The family made and sold more such boxes and then started a line of seashells and a variety of other seashell novelties. The store became known as the Shell Shop. A few years later, it added a sideline: barreled kerosene. By the dawn of the automotive age in 1900, the focus of the expanding company was on oil and gasoline. In 1904, it adopted the scalloped seashell as its logo.

SHRAPNEL ■ In 1804, when British troops invaded Surinam (then called Guiana) in South America, they used a new type of anti-personnel artillery shell. Inside, it was packed not only with powder but also with metal balls, and the whole of it was set off by a time fuse so that it would explode in midair and scatter the shot with tremendous force over a wide area. The new type of shell played a key roll in the British victory in Surinam and later, in 1815, at the battle of Waterloo.

The shell was the invention of Colonel Henry Shrapnel. When he passed away in 1942, it was with a long-held grudge against the British government. Despite years of claims and protests, he had never been able to convince the bureaucrats that he should be compensated for the money he had taken from his own pocket to develop the shell.

Today the word *shrapnel* refers to any kind of bullets, darts, or scrap metal scattered by high explosives.

SHREDDED WHEAT ▪ Businessman Henry Perkey of Denver had a sensitive stomach. One morning in the early 1890s, he was in a hotel dining room having a breakfast of whole boiled wheat with milk. As he chewed, the idea came to him that the wheat would be a lot easier to eat and digest if it was shredded. By 1893, Mr. Perky was making and selling Shredded Wheat, the first ready-to-eat breakfast cereal.

But then came problems. Competitors began copying the product and using the name *Shredded Wheat* on their own boxes. In lawsuits that followed, the Shredded Wheat Co. lost—for the reason that, at that time, descriptive words such as *shredded* could not be in the brand name. As a result, for a year (1941) the brand was called Welgar, an acronym for the location of its head office at Welwyn Garden City. By 1943, the name had again been changed—to Nabisco Shredded Wheat. *Nabisco* itself is an acronym for the National Biscuit Company.

(See Breakfast Cereal, page 18.)

SIDEBURNS ▪ When he was a kid, Ambrose Burnside loved to read about military heroes and battles of the past—and dreamed of someday becoming a soldier. His dream came true. In fact, he grew up to be a Union general in the Civil War, one with great,

During the Civil War, Burnside sent his army across a river on crude pontoon bridges. More than nine hundred of his soldiers were slaughtered and a special truce had to be called so that they could be buried.

bushy whiskers flanking his face. He was very courageous but usually managed to foul up every battle he fought. Regardless, some men started copying what were at first called Burnside whiskers. In popular usage, the words switched places and became *sideburns*.

"SILENT NIGHT" ■ The church organ broke down on Christmas Eve, 1818, in a little town in Austria. That inspired the organist to rapidly come up with words for a hymn that the choir could sing without musical accompaniment. By candlelight, with quill and ink, he wrote *"Stille Nacht"* on that unusually silent night.

SILHOUETTE ■ Before cameras were in common use, silhouettes were as popular (and cheap) as snapshots. Silhouette artists, highly skilled in the freehand use of scissors, would fold a piece of black paper and then cut the shadow outline of a person's head or figure.

> *Heaping on the ridicule, some pants were made à la Silhouette—that is, without pockets—the suggestion being that Silhouette, by taking everyone's money, had made pockets unnecessary.*

Étienne de Silhouette (1709–1767) wasn't known for his paper-and-scissors skill. Instead, when he became the French director of finances (1757), rich people hated him for seizing their assets and poor people hated him for imposing crushing new taxes. Because the French thought he was a stingy, shady figure, they made fun of him by referring to the cheap, dark cutouts of people as silhouettes.

SIREN ■ In Greek mythology, the Sirens were beautiful creatures—part bird, part woman. They lived by the sea, luring sailors to their deaths on rocky coastlines by singing loud, enchanting songs. It is from this mythology that the modern siren (a beautiful, seductive woman) gets her name.

SKI ■ The word *ski* comes from the old Norwegian word *skīdh,* meaning "strip of wood." Pronounced *shee,* it is also the Scandinavian term for *snowshoe.*

According to experts, the first skis were made from the flat, curving rib bones of large animals. Later came wooden skis made from flat strips of pine, spruce, or ash. To make them slide better over the surface of the snow, some early skis were covered with hardened leather. Other skis had wooden strips or runners along the bottom.

SMITHSONIAN INSTITUTION ■ The Smithsonian Institution in Washington, D.C., is by far the largest and most incredible museum complex in the United States. And the story behind its founder and namesake is one of the strangest riddles in American history.

> *In 1904, Smithson's body was shipped to the United States and interred in a vault in the Administration Building of the museum.*

James Smithson was a wealthy Englishman born in France in 1765. During his lifetime, he never set foot in the United States. And as far as we know, he never so much as wrote a letter to anyone in the country, since he did not have any American relatives, friends, or even business acquaintances. When his will was read after his death in 1829, Smithson's family and friends were completely shocked to learn that he had left a fortune to the United States to build a monument to American history that was "to be known as the Smithsonian Institution."

> *If Smithson's nephew Henry Hungerford had not died before Smithson, the money would have gone to the young man, not to the United States.*

The Smithsonian was not founded until 1846. Incredibly, when the money was first offered, Congress deliberated for *eight* years before deciding to accept it! One senator of the time declared: "[If we establish this museum] every whippersnapper vagabond . . . might think it proper to have his name distinguished in the same way."

The Smithsonian museums welcome millions of visitors each year and display such artifacts as World War I machine guns; the ruby slippers worn by Judy Garland in *The Wizard of Oz*; dresses of America's First Ladies; and *Apollo II*, the lunar module that landed on the moon in 1969.

SMOKEY THE BEAR ■ His original name was Hot Foot Teddy. When he was found in New Mexico in 1950 by forest rangers, his mother had been killed and his paws had been badly burned in a massive forest fire. Shortly after his recovery, his name was changed to Smokey the Bear, and he became a national symbol of the importance of fire prevention.

SNOB ▪ Today's snobs think they're better than everybody else. Noses snootily raised, they attach great importance to their money, looks, and social position. Over the centuries, the word went through a strange reversal of meaning. A *snob,* originally, was an ill-kempt slob—a dolt, a not-too-bright member of the lowest class.

SNORKEL ▪ People have been snorkeling since ancient times. The first tubes for breathing underwater were hollow reeds. Later came J-shaped tubes of glass, metal, rubber, and eventually plastic.

Though the idea of the snorkel is old, the word is a pretty new one. During World War II, German U-boats were equipped with extra-big air pipes. Sailors jokingly referred to the things as *schnorkels* because of the snoring noises they made and because they looked like schnozzes— slang for "snouts, big noses."

SOAP OPERA ▪ These melodramas were first broadcast on radio in the 1930s and were only fifteen minutes long. Because they always dealt with "unseemly romance," tragedy, and "other unpleasantness," for the first few years of the industry, it was a rule that they be sponsored by "wholesome products," which in almost all cases was soap.

SOCCER ▪ Soccer is the parent game of all forms of football, from Canadian and American football to Rugby. In Rugby, players can run with the ball or lateral it (toss it sideways); in the American and Canadian games, there are set plays in which the players can run or pass the ball; in soccer, the ball can only be kicked or hit with various parts of the body.

In 1863, the London Football Association of England laid out the rules for soccer. For this reason, for a time it was known as association football. Then the name *soccer* was created from the word *association*—or, to be more exact, from its second syllable, *soc*.

(See Rugby, page 99.)

SOFA ▪ Once upon a time, if you sat on a sofa, you were going for a ride on a camel! The word *sofa* originally referred to a fancy cushion on a camel's saddle.

SPAIN ▪ The Spanish owe the name of their nation to the people of Carthage, a North African state. In the 6th century, they named it Spania, meaning "the Land of Rabbits."

SPAM® ▪ At first, the name on the can was SPICED HAM. Looking for a shorter, snappier name, the company held a contest, offering $100 to the winner. *BRUNCH* almost came in first, but the winning entry ended up being *SPAM*. The brother of one of the company's vice-presidents suggested the name, a combination of *spiced* and *ham*.

How did the word *spam* become the name for unwanted messages that find their way into your computer's electronic mailbox? In a 1970s comedy skit featured on a TV show called *Monty Python's Flying Circus,* a restaurant serves lots of SPAM, and the word is repeated an annoying number of times. Because of this skit, the meaning of the word became linked to something that's done over and over—like repeatedly sending the same unwanted email, often an advertisement. Mass emails were first called spam in 1993.

The new SPAM Museum was opened in Austin, Minnesota, in 2001 to celebrate the "unprecedented excitement SPAM has inspired."

In 2002, Hormel Foods produced the six-billionth can of SPAM.

STAGECOACH ▪ How come it was called a stagecoach? Because travel by means of these horse-drawn coaches took place in stages—over a period of days, sometimes weeks, with stops at inns and taverns along the way.

Stagecoaches first began appearing in England and Europe in the 17th century. Travel by stagecoach reached its height of popularity in the United States during the mid-19th century in the Old West.

"STAR-SPANGLED BANNER, THE" ■ Originally entitled "The Defense of Fort McHenry," the song that eventually became the U.S. national anthem was written by a lawyer named Francis Scott Key in 1814. Imprisoned aboard a British warship, Key and other American prisoners watched the battle rage all day and night. Even when dawn came, Key and his fellow prisoners couldn't tell who had won the battle because of smoke and fog. But then a sudden break in the gray shroud revealed the American flag still flying over the walls of the fort. Exhilarated, filled with pride, Key felt compelled to put his feelings on paper. He pulled a half-written letter from his pocket and started writing, completing most of the song in a few minutes.

"The Star-Spangled Banner" did not become our national anthem until 1931.

> Oh! say, can you see, by the dawn's early light,
> What so proudly we hailed at the twilight's last gleaming?
> Whose broad stripes and bright stars, thro' the perilous fight,
> O'er the ramparts we watched were so gallantly streaming?
> And the rocket's red glare, the bombs bursting in air,
> Gave proof thro' the night that our flag was still there.
> Oh! say, does that star-spangled banner yet wave
> O'er the land of the free and the home of the brave?

STATE NAMES ■ ALABAMA (HEART OF DIXIE) • This state is named after the Alabama River, which got its name from the Alibamon, a tribe of the Choctaw Nation that lived along its banks.

ALASKA (THE LAST FRONTIER) • The largest of the fifty United States, Alaska originally was known as Russian America. When it was purchased from Russia by the United States in 1867 (for $7.2 million), it was renamed Alaska. The name is an adaptation of the Aleutian (Inuit) word *Alakshak,* meaning "the great country" or "land that is not an island."

The amount paid for Alaska comes out to only 2 cents per acre!
Purchase of the land was largely the work of Secretary of State William Seward (1801–1872). Though Alaska has proved to be extremely valuable to the United States, at the time it was called "Seward's Folly" and "Seward's Icebox."

ARIZONA (GRAND CANYON STATE) • The state's name comes from the Pima Indian word *arizonac,* meaning "land of few springs."

ARKANSAS (THE NATURAL STATE) • In 1673, Father Jacques Marquette, a Catholic priest, learned of a Native American tribe whose name was pronounced *Oo-ka-na-sa* and meant "downstream people." Over the next two centuries, explorers and settlers referred to the entire region by this name. The problem was, everybody spelled it differently: Arkensa, Arkancas, and Arkansas, for example. This last spelling—Arkansas—was adopted when the state was admitted to the Union in 1836.

In 1881, a legislative committee was formed to determine the correct pronunciation of the last syllable, which it ultimately concluded should be Ark-an-SAW.

CALIFORNIA (GOLDEN STATE) • Believe it or not, California was named for an imaginary place in a 16th-century Spanish novel, *The Exploits of Esplandian,* by Garcia Montalvo. The place was an evil kingdom, an island made of gigantic rocks.

In the book, Esplandian, a good knight, goes to California and finds it inhabited by huge Amazonian women ruled by the wicked Queen Califa. After the queen fights a duel with Esplandian and gets trounced, she and her subjects convert to Christianity.

California was once a country. Protesting a tax on gold, for a three-month period in 1850 (ten years before the Civil War) it seceded from the Union and became a separate nation.

The novel was a favorite of Hernán Cortés, who, in his explorations of the New World, named California in memory of the place imagined by Montalvo.

Why is North Carolina nicknamed the Tar Heel State? In the early days of its statehood, workers used pitch and tar made from pine sap to waterproof their wooden ships. One story claims that workers got tar on their feet as they worked and were called Tar Heels. The name stuck!

CAROLINA (NORTH and SOUTH) • The sister states are named after King Charles I of England. As was the custom, the male name (Carolus, the Latin form of Charles) was changed to its feminine form (Carolina). North Carolina is nicknamed the Tar Heel State. South Carolina is called the Palmetto State.

COLORADO (CENTENNIAL STATE) • Spanish explorers of the 16th century called the area Colorado ("colored red") because of the pigment in the soil. In 1859, it was known as the U.S. Territory of Jefferson, after the third U.S. president. In 1860, it was known briefly as Idaho, but the territory was soon renamed, using the original Spanish word—*Colorado*.

Colorado has more mountains over 14,000 feet high, and more elk, than any other state.

(See Idaho, page 112.)

CONNECTICUT (CONSTITUTION STATE) • Named for the Connecticut River, an Algonquian word meaning "on the long river tide."

DAKOTA (NORTH and SOUTH) • The states are named after the Dakota Indians. *Dakota* means "think [of all] as friends." In 1889, the Dakota Territory was divided into two states, North and South Dakota. North Dakota is nicknamed the Peace Garden State. South Dakota is called the Mount Rushmore State.

DELAWARE (FIRST STATE) • In 1610, an English nobleman, Lord De La Warr, hired another Englishman, Captain Samuel Argall, to explore a vast river system in northeastern America. The captain named the river, the state, and even the Native American tribe in the area after the nobleman who had hired him.

FLORIDA (SUNSHINE STATE) • Explorer Ponce de León first set foot on this large peninsula in 1513 on the day of a festival called *El Pascua Florida,* meaning "flowery Easter." And, because of its climate, the place was indeed very green and flowery *(florido)*.

GEORGIA (PEACH STATE) • In 1732, King George II of England granted James Oglethorpe a royal charter to a large piece of land in the southeast region of what is now the United

The name George means "farmer."

States. As a show of appreciation, Oglethorpe named the region after the king. Following the custom, he changed the name into its feminine form—from *George* to *Georgia.*

Alabama and Mississippi were carved out of western Georgia.

HAWAII (ALOHA STATE) • The state's name derives from the Polynesian word *Hawaiki,* the name of the traditional homeland of the Polynesian people.

In 1778, Captain James Cook of England became the first European to set foot on the islands. In honor of his patron, the Earl of Sandwich, he called them the Sandwich Islands, by which name they were known for many years. In 1959, Hawaii became the fiftieth state of the Union. In all, it is made up of 122 islands.

Q: What is the only state that ends in three vowels?

A: Hawaii

IDAHO (GEM STATE) • This state's name doesn't mean a thing. Here's what happened. When a name was needed in 1860 for a territory in the Pike's Peak mining area, George M. Willing, an eccentric character, suggested the "Indian" word *idaho.* "It means 'gem of the mountains,'" claimed Willing. Just as Congress was going through the motions of adopting the name, Willing laughed and said he'd just been kidding around. "Made the name up, as a joke," he admitted.

A red-faced Congress went for its second choice: *Colorado* (the original Spanish word for the area).

Two years later, it came time to name another mining territory, this one in the Pacific Northwest. Wackily, once again the name *Idaho* was suggested. Either not knowing or caring that the name had started out as a joke, the people—and their representatives in Congress—liked the sound of it. In 1863, Idaho became a U.S. territory; in 1890, it became a state.

(See Colorado, page 111.)

ILLINOIS (PRAIRIE STATE) • In the 17th century, French explorers traveling down the Mississippi River found themselves in a region inhabited by the people of a strong, populous Algonquin nation. When the Native American leaders were asked who they were, they replied that they were "men"—*illiniwek*. And they were "warriors"—*ileni*. As a result, the French called the territory Illinois and the people the Illini. In 1867, when students at the University of Illinois nicknamed themselves the Fighting Illini, they gave new life (and a new spelling) to the Algonquin tribe's word for *warriors*.

INDIANA (HOOSIER STATE) • Indiana is a Latin word meaning "land of the Indians." The name was first used in 1768 by the Philadelphus Trading Company to identify territory ceded to them by the Iroquois Indians.

IOWA (HAWKEYE STATE) • The Dakota Indians sneeringly referred to various tribes occupying territory to the south of them as the Ayuba, the "sleepy one." *Ayuba,* garbled in translation, became *Iowa*.

KANSAS (SUNFLOWER STATE) • The state is named for the Kansa, or Kaw, Indians who once lived in the region. The word means "people of the south wind."

The first newspaper in Kansas was written in the language of the Shawnee Indians.

ı the War of 1812, more than half { all Americans killed in action ere Kentuckians.

KENTUCKY (BLUEGRASS STATE) • This state's name comes from a Huron Indian word meaning "dark and bloody ground." Native American tribes had lived in the region—and fought for it—for more than fourteen hundred years, until the arrival of European explorers in the 16th century.

LOUISIANA (PELICAN STATE) • The state was named in 1682 after King Louis XIV of France.

Eighteen French kings were named Louis.

MAINE (PINE TREE STATE) • This state was a part of Massachusetts for almost two hundred years, a part that people referred to as the "mainland." Mainlanders got more and more fed up with being a part of Massachusetts. They resented the fact that the state government taxed them heavily but provided almost no services, such as decent roads. In 1820, the large region broke with Massachusetts and, taking the first half of its nickname with it, became the state of Maine.

MARYLAND (OLD LINE STATE, FREE STATE) • When Charles I of England took the throne in 1625, he was in love with a French princess named Maria. His counselor demanded that he take an English girl as his queen. Shocking Europe, he married the fifteen-year-old French girl; and with her name in the Anglican form, she became Queen Mary of England. It is after the heroine of this fairy-tale-like story that Maryland takes its name.

MASSACHUSETTS (BAY STATE) • Massachusetts' name comes from the Algonquin words *massa,* meaning "great," and *wachuset,* meaning "hill."

> *The first income tax in U.S. history was imposed in New Plymouth, Massachusetts, in 1643.*

MICHIGAN (GREAT LAKES STATE) • Michigan is named after Lake Michigan, which derives from the Chippewa word *michigama,* meaning "great water."

MINNESOTA (NORTH STAR STATE) • Minnesota's name comes from the Sioux Indian word *menesota,* meaning "cloudy water."

> *Sicily is an island off the southern coast of Italy (and part of that country). In 1947, representatives of Sicily asked President Harry S Truman to make it a state, "the forty-ninth American star."*

MISSISSIPPI (MAGNOLIA STATE) • This state is named after the Mississippi River, which takes its name from the Algonquin words *meeche* (meaning "great") and *cebe* ("river"). The French explorer who first wrote down the name spelled it *Michi Sepe.*

MISSOURI (SHOW ME STATE) • The state was named after the Missouri River, which in turn was named after the Missouri Indians, one of the tribes that lived near its mouth. The name means "the town of large canoes."

MONTANA (TREASURE STATE) • *Montana* is the Spanish word for "mountain," with an English pronunciation.

NEBRASKA (CORNHUSKER STATE) • The name *Nebraska* is the result of people having trouble communicating with one another. In the 1700s, European explorers, trying to find out the name of the region, asked Oto Indians what it was called. *"Nebrathka,"* replied the Indians. The name, which means "flat water," however, referred to the main river flowing through the region (the Platte), not the land.

NEVADA (SILVER STATE, BATTLE BORN STATE) • *Nevada* is a Spanish word meaning "snow-covered," in reference to the many white-topped peaks of the Sierra Nevada mountain range.

NEW HAMPSHIRE (GRANITE STATE) • Captain John Mason named this state in 1629 to honor his home county of Hampshire, England.

NEW JERSEY (GARDEN STATE) • In 55 B.C., during the Roman conquest of England, the largest island in the English Channel was named Caesar. Over the centuries, the English garbled and slurred the name to *Jersey*.

Long known for the high quality of its knitted products, the island also lent its name to an item in your wardrobe— to any jersey you might own.

When American colonists named New Jersey after the British island, it's unlikely that any of them realized the state's name derived from that of the Roman emperor.

NEW MEXICO (LAND OF ENCHANTMENT) • Spanish explorer Francisco de Ibarra named this state in 1562 in honor of his former homeland, Mexico.

NEW YORK (EMPIRE STATE) • New York was named after the Duke of York (1633–1701), who later became King James II of England.

OHIO (BUCKEYE STATE) • Ohio gets its name from the Iroquois word *oheo,* meaning "beautiful."

OKLAHOMA (SOONER STATE) • This state name is a compound of two Choctaw Indian words, *okla* (people) and *homma* (red). Thus, the name means "land of the red people." Oklahoma's nickname—Sooner State—refers to what were called "land runs," held in the 1800s in various territories before Oklahoma was a state. A land run was a kind of competition to claim a piece of land before anyone else could. At the sound of a shotgun, thousands of competitors would race to put stakes in the ground, marking where they wanted to build their houses. The name "sooner" was used for those land runners who sneaked past the territory markers prior to the actual shotgun start to claim the best areas. They were those who claimed land "sooner"!

OREGON (BEAVER STATE) • In 1792, Captain Robert Gray sailed up a large river, which he called Columbia, after his ship. Later explorers learned that Native Americans called the river the *ore-gon,* meaning "beautiful water." The Oregon Territory took its name from that of the river, as did the state, in 1859.

PENNSYLVANIA (KEYSTONE STATE) • King Charles II of England (1630–1685) owed William Penn the Younger sixteen thousand pounds. Instead of the money, Penn asked the king for land in America for followers of his faith, the Society of Friends, commonly known as Quakers. The land Penn asked for was to be a

Quakers believe in simple speech and dress, consider all war to be wrong, and feel that oaths and rituals are of no value.

refuge for the Quakers, a place where they could be safe from persecutors—people who tormented, and even killed, them just because of their beliefs. The king exchanged the land for the money and then named it Penn's Sylvania, not after William Penn the Younger but after his father, William Penn the Elder, a British admiral and friend of the king. As for *Sylvania,* it means "a place in the forest." Thus, the state is Admiral Penn's Forest.

(See Quaker Oats®, page 95.)

RHODE ISLAND (THE OCEAN STATE) • In 1524, Italian navigator Giovanni da Verrazano was looking for a way to sail his ship through

The isle of Rhodes—and thus Rhode Island as well—takes its name from the Rhodes, a medieval order of knights that once occupied the island.

America to China. Instead, he found what would, 120 years later, become the state of Rhode Island. Verrazano himself named the place Luisa. But when he wrote to

A strange little twist: The first settlers (1636) were actually on the wrong island, one that the Native Americans called Aquidneck. It's Aquidneck that became Rhode Island, not the island Verrazano saw.

the people financing the expedition that Luisa reminded him of the isle of Rhodes in the Mediterranean, they decided to rename it Rhode Island.

Rhode Island's official name is State of Rhode Island and Providence Plantations. The smallest state has the longest name!

For four years (1784–1788) the United States had a state called Franklin! Named after Ben Franklin, it was in what today is a mountainous part of Tennessee.

TENNESSEE (VOLUNTEER STATE) • Tennessee's name derives from *Tanasi,* which was originally the name of a Cherokee village.

Why is Tennessee nicknamed the Volunteer State? During the Mexican-American War (1846–1848), when men across the United States were called upon to join up, the response from Tennessee was amazing: more than thirty thousand men signed up to fight.

TEXAS (LONE STAR STATE) • The name comes from the Native American word *techas,* meaning, "friends/allies." The Techas was an alliance of tribes that united to fight the fierce Apaches.

To this day, Texas has the legal right to divide itself into as many as five states.

UTAH (BEEHIVE STATE) • Deseret—that's the original name given to the state by Mormon settlers. Later, the name was changed to Utah, meaning, "land of the Utes." The Utes are a Native American tribe whose name translates as "the hill dwellers."

VERMONT (GREEN MOUNTAIN STATE) • The nickname refers to the evergreen forests of its mountains. Vermont's name is derived from the combination of two French words: *vert,* which means "green," and *mont,* meaning "mountain."

VIRGINIA (OLD DOMINION) • Virginia is named after Queen Elizabeth I of England, who, because she refused to marry, came to be known as the Virgin Queen.

Originally, Virginia included most of the eastern United States and all of western America. When the English established the colony, the Pacific Ocean was designated as Virginia's western boundary!

WASHINGTON (EVERGREEN STATE) • Nine states are named after European royalty. Only one is named after a president—Washington. It almost didn't make it. Originally, the name was going to be Columbia, until one congressman argued that the name would always be confused with the District of Columbia (Washington, D.C.). Since the capital of the United States and this North Pacific state are both referred to as Washington, it all turned out to be very confusing anyway.

The results of the West Virginia Vote are questionable. Union troops were stationed at many of the polls to prevent Confederate sympathizers from voting!

WEST VIRGINIA (MOUNTAIN STATE) • The area was part of Virginia until the time of the Civil War (1861–1865). When Virginia voted to secede, the western counties objected strongly and chose to remain loyal to the Union. To do so, in 1863, West Virginia became a separate state.

Q: What's the only letter not used in the spelling of any of the fifty state names?

A: Q

WISCONSIN (BADGER STATE) • Wisconsin's name comes from the Ojibwa Indian word *wees-kon-san,* meaning "the gathering of the waters."

WYOMING (EQUALITY STATE, COWBOY STATE) • The state's name comes from the last three syllables of the Indian word *miche-weaming,* meaning, "at the big plains."

Yellowstone National Park, located in Wyoming, Idaho, and Montana, was the world's first national park, established in 1872. There are more geysers and hot springs there than in the rest of the world combined.

STATUE OF LIBERTY ■ In 1856, French diplomat and engineer Ferdinand-Marie de Lesseps began work on a fantastic plan. By means of a long canal through Egypt, he would join the Red Sea and the Mediterranean. More than ten years later, his dream came true. Today, his waterway is known as the Suez Canal.

During construction of the canal, French sculptor Frédéric-Auguste Bartholdi was greatly inspired. He hoped to build a huge lighthouse—a statue of a colossal robed woman—at the entrance to the canal. Torch in hand, one arm would be raised in greeting.

Alexandre-Gustave Eiffel, creator of the Eiffel Tower, also engineered the construction of the Statue of Liberty.

Though people loved the idea—and Bartholdi's design—nobody would come up with the money to pay for it. After more than a decade of trying, Bartholdi returned from Egypt to France. The Suez Canal was complete, but his beautiful statue remained only a design on paper.

The pedestal for the Statue of Liberty was more expensive than Lady Liberty herself.

A few years later, Bartholdi found financial backing—but not to build his statue at the entrance to the Suez Canal. Instead, his French backers (our allies in what was then known as the Franco-American Union) decided to have the statue placed at the entrance to New York Harbor, where it could stand as a symbol of democracy. Much of the money donated for it came from French schoolchildren. Built in France, the statue was shipped across the Atlantic in 214 crates and then reassembled in New York on Liberty Island, where it stands today.

Bartholdi's monument could have been built at the entrance to the Suez Canal. It could have had a different name. With a few minor twists in history, it would have been the Statue of Suez. Instead, we know it today as the Statue of Liberty.

STEELERS, Pittsburgh (NFL) ■ When the football team was founded in 1933, Art Rooney, Sr., its owner, named it the Pirates, after his favorite baseball team. The team remained the Pirates until 1940, when Rooney renamed it the Steelers. The name represented the city's heritage as one of the largest and greatest makers of steel.

(See Pirates, Pittsburgh, page 90, and Eagles, Philadelphia, page 41.)

STEVIE WONDER ■ His real name is Steveland Judkins Morris. When he recorded his first national hit "Fingertips," at the age of twelve, his promoter called him "Little Stevie Wonder." Though blinded in infancy due to lack of proper oxygen flow to his incubator, he has never considered himself disabled. "I did what all the kids my age were doing," Stevie has said. "I played games, rode bikes, climbed trees—and I loved to sing!"

STING ■ Gordon Matthew Sumner, an ex-teacher, received the nickname Sting while he was a member of the Phoenix Jazzmen. Every member of the rock group had a nickname. One day, Sumner came to a rehearsal in a black-and-yellow striped soccer sweater. Gordon Solomon, the trombone player, remarked that the singer looked like a bee. This led to him being called Stinger, which eventually became Sting.

In 1977, the group changed its name to the Police, with Sting as the lead singer and bass guitarist. The Police didn't get along, with members occasionally slugging it out. In 1986, Sting took off on his own.

SUEDE ■ *Suede* is tanned leather, usually from a calf, with the flesh side turned out and buffed very smooth and soft. It was first produced in Sweden, the French name for which is *Suede.*

SUPER BOWL ■ The Super Bowl was named after a toy, the Super Ball. It happened one day in 1967. . . .

A young girl named Sharon Hunt was in her Texas home, bouncing a Super Ball around. Made of a secret compound called Zectron, and with six times the bounce of ordinary rubber, the ball caught the attention of Sharon's dad, who asked what the name of it was.

It so happened that Sharon's father, Lamar Hunt, was the owner of the Kansas City Chiefs of the NFL. A few days later, he and the other owners got together for a meeting. One of the most important items on the agenda was a new name for what had, for its first two years, been called the AFL-NFL World Championship Game. Instead of this long, boring mouthful of words, something shorter and livelier was needed. At first nothing came to mind. But then Mr. Hunt thought of Sharon and her Super Ball. He blurted out a slightly changed name, *Super Bowl,* and that has been its name ever since.

SUPERMAN ■ While in high school in the 1930s, teenager Jerry Siegel wrote a story for his English class entitled "The Reign of Superman," about a villain with extraordinary powers. Siegel and his artist buddy Joe

Born on the dying planet Krypton in the city of Kandor, Superman's name at birth was Kal-El.

Shuster turned it into a comic-book character (about a *hero* with extraordinary powers). All of the "big," well-known companies turned down the comic book. Action Comics, a small, fledgling company at the time, picked it up—and Superman appeared in the first edition of *Action Comics* in June 1938. Superman soon became the best-selling superhero in the country, and several movies based on his adventures became blockbuster hits.

SURNAMES (last names) ■ Until the Middle Ages, most people had only a first name. But as the population grew, so did the need to further identify individuals. (In medieval England, three out of every five men were named Tom, John, Henry, William, Edward, or Richard.) A last name was needed to make it clear who you were talking about.

Chang is the most common family name in the world.

Smith is the most common in the United States and Britain.

THE FOUR MOST COMMON WAYS LAST NAMES WERE CREATED:

1. OCCUPATIONAL—What a person did for a living often became his or her last name. For example, a person known as Mary, the Baker, eventually became Mary Baker. Shoemaker, Carpenter, Horseman, Singer, and Butler are among hundreds of other "job" names.

2. PATRONYMIC—A father's name plus *son*. For example, Michael, John's son, became Michael Johnson. A few others: Richardson, Stevenson, Davidson, Wilson, Jackson.

    A father's name *without son*. For example, Linda, Edward's daughter, would eventually become known as Linda Edwards. More examples: Johns, Michaels, Holmes, and Phillips.

Johnson is the second most common—followed in order by Williams, Brown, Jones, Miller, Davis, Wilson, Anderson, and Taylor.

3. DESCRIPTIVE—Many last names describe some characteristic of the person—names such as Little, Browne, Elder, Younger, Long, and White.

4. PLACE NAMES—Words that described where a

Garcia is the most common surname in Spain, Mexico, and Central and South America.

person lived—Tom of the Woods eventually became Tom Woods. (Not to be confused with Tom Marsh, Tom Glen, Tom Rivers, or Tom Hill, etc.)

SUSPENDERS ■ Invented in 18th-century England, at first they were called gallowses, so named because, like execution gallows of the time, they were used for "hanging." Weirdly, these first ever suspenders were very short—they pulled up a man's pants almost all the way to his armpits!

Today in England, they are called braces. In Mexico and other Spanish-speaking countries, they are called *tirantes de pantaloon,* "pants pullers." In the United States, they're suspenders—straps from which pants are "suspended." The word *suspenders* didn't enter the English language until the 19th century.

TAE KWON DO ■ Tae kwon do evolved from an earlier Korean form of self-defense called *soo bak* (meaning "punching and head butting"). The name *tae kwon do* means "the way of the hand and foot" and involves hitting, kicking, and head butting.

Tae kwon do became popular in the United States after soldiers returned from the Korean War (1950–1953), bringing their new martial arts skills with them. During the 1960s, this style of karate became internationally known.

(See Judo, page 65; Karate, page 66.)

TANKS ■ In 1914, the British began secretly designing and building armored military vehicles. For security purposes,
mechanics and others working on the
weapons were told to tell people they
were making "water carriers" and other
kinds of "tanks."

TANTALIZE ■ To be *tantalized* is to get close to something you desire terribly
and then have it kept from you. It is to be filled with hope one moment and disappointment the next. The word comes from a Greek myth.

Tantalus, the king of Lydia, an ancient city in western Asia Minor, invited the
gods to dine with him. To test their divinity, he served the body of his own son.
One god, Demeter, took a large bite out of the shoulder. Instantly, the gods knew
what Tantalus had done. Zeus brought the boy back to life, replacing his shoulder
with one of ivory.

For his crime, Tantalus was cast into hell. He stood waist deep in the middle
of a lake, surrounded by trees heavy with delicious fruit. Thirst and hunger
that he could never satisfy tortured him: When he reached out his hand, the
fruit always rose just beyond reach; when he leaned down to drink, the water
receded.

TARZAN ■ Tarzan is the hero of an extremely popular series of adventure stories
written by Edgar Rice Burroughs in the early 20th century, later dramatized in
movies and featured in a syndicated comic-strip serial. In the stories, Tarzan is a
white boy who has been raised among apes in the African jungle. What does the
name *Tarzan* mean? In the complete ape language that Burroughs created, *tar*
means "white" and *zan* means "skin."

TEA ■ According to legend, in 2737 B.C., Chinese emperor Shen Nung was boiling water when leaves from a nearby bush drifted down into the pot. He found
that this created a pleasant-tasting beverage, which he named after the shrub, the
t'e plant.

"TEN MOST WANTED" CRIMINALS ■ In 1950, J. Edgar Hoover, the director of the FBI, began the practice of issuing a list of the "Ten Most Wanted." A friend, a fashion designer who invented the survey of the "Ten Best Dressed Women," suggested the idea to him.

TENNIS ■ The name *tennis* comes from the French exclamation *tenez!* Loosely translated, *tenez* means "get ready, I'm gonna serve!"

TENNIS SHOES ■ The first canvas-and-rubber shoes were made in the United States in 1876 for playing croquet. They weren't called croquet shoes; instead they were known as plimsolls, taking their name from Samuel Plimsoll, a popular English politician of the time who liked wearing them. They consisted of a rubber sole attached to brown canvas, contrary to the fact that sports shoes, until that time, had been made of brown leather with rubber soles. In 1874, tennis began to be played in America. Plimsolls were found to be ideally suited for the game—and they've been known as tennis shoes happily ever after.

In tennis, the term love means "zero." (For example, the score of a game might be 3–love.) The term came about because the shape of a zero—0—resembles an egg, and in French, l'oeuf means both "egg" and "zero." When pronounced in English, l'oeuf sounded like love.

(See Adidas, page 4, and Nike, page 79.)

TESTIMONY ■ In ancient Rome, only men were allowed to speak in court. According to Roman law, the man had to place his right hand over his testicles while taking an oath to tell the truth to the court. His version of the events came to be known as his sworn testimony (or in Latin, *testimonium*).

The custom of the groom carrying the bride over the threshold goes back to medieval times. It symbolizes the strength of the man and his ability to take care of his wife. As for the woman, it shows that she is valued highly and treated like a princess.

THRESHOLD ■ In the Middle Ages, the floor of a house was usually hard-packed dirt covered with straw, then called thresh. The *threshold* was a wooden beam to hold the straw—the thresh—back and keep it from going out the door.

THUG ■ In India in the 19th century, a *thug* was a member of a fanatical religious sect made up of professional assassins, the *thugees*. Members of the sect hated all the wealthy foreigners coming into their country at the time. Thugs followed the foreigners, mostly British and other Europeans, and then strangled and robbed them. The thugs killed not only for the money, but also to show their devotion to Kali, the Hindu goddess of destruction—or so they claimed.

Tonka® Trucks ■ In 1946, three friends—Avery Crounse, Lynn Baker, and Alvin Tesch—founded the Metalcraft Company in the basement of a Minnesota schoolhouse. At first, they manufactured garden tools—rakes, pitchforks, and shovels. When the business failed, they decided to make toys. A toy steam shovel was first; then came trucks, forklifts, fire engines, and other vehicles. The three partners called their new company Tonka, naming it after nearby Lake Minnetonka. By itself, the Sioux Indian word *tonka* means "great."

Tootsie Roll® ■ Leo Hirschfield, an Austrian immigrant to the United States, was a candy maker. One day in 1896, he came up with a new, original candy, one that had to be rolled by hand. The first person ever to try it was his daughter, whose nickname was Tootsie.

The Tootsie Roll was the first commercially produced candy wrapped in paper.

TRADITION ■ The word *tradition* (spelled *traditio* in Latin, and later *tradicion* in French and *tradycion* in English) originally meant "to betray, to be a traitor."

TRIVIA ■ The word *trivia* comes from the Latin for "crossroads": *tri+via,* meaning "three streets." At Roman crossroads, travelers left messages for one another. These brief items of interest came to be known as trivia.

TULIP ■ The Christian Crusaders (11th to 14th centuries) referred to the tulip as the Rose of Sharon. To the people of Turkey, the flower resembled a turban, so they called it by the Turkish name for that garment—*tülbend*. The Italians translated this as *tulipano,* which became *tulipe* in French and finally ended up in English as *tulip*.

TURTLE and TORTOISE ■ Turtles live in water. Tortoises live on land. Both get their name from the Latin word for a mythological demon the Greeks called Tartarouchos. Its body was twisted together strangely and horribly, and it lived in the ultimate prison, a second underworld—a hell below hell.

Turtle Wax® ■ In 1941, Ben and Marie Hirsch formulated the world's first liquid car polish: Plastone. Together, they opened a small business. Ben used the bathtub to mix batches of the polish; Marie was in charge of bottling and labeling. Ben peddled Plastone to gas stations and garage owners in the Midwest. Sometimes he would hand-polish the fender of a parked car and then wait for the owner to return to make a sale! On his way home from a sales trip to Wisconsin, he passed through a small town called Turtle Creek. Thinking of his product as a protective shell, he renamed it (with Marie's blessing) Super Hard Shell Turtle Wax.

TUXEDO ■ In the 19th century, it was customary for gentlemen to wear a fancy black "swallow-tailed" garment, usually referred to as tails, to formal social events. In the summer of 1886, Pierre Lorillard IV decided he wanted to wear something less formal to the annual Autumn Ball. He hired a tailor to prepare several tail-less black jackets. On the night of the ball, Pierre lost his nerve and wore tails instead. But his son, Griswold, and several of the young man's friends donned the new garments. The suits soon became known as tuxedos. Why? The Autumn Ball of 1886 was held in a small town in New York State, a place called Tuxedo Park.

TWAIN, MARK ■ Samuel Langhorne Clemens (1835–1910), the American author best known for *Tom Sawyer* and *The Adventures of Huckleberry Finn,* was a ship's captain on a Mississippi riverboat from 1859 to 1861. On the boats he piloted, a leadsman dangled a weighted length of twine into the water and called out the depth to the captain to prevent the ship from running aground. "Mark on the twine, two fathoms!" would have been a common call. With a southern drawl, this sounded like "mark twain," which Clemens adopted as his pen name.

An umbrella with a handle that concealed a sword was found in King Tut's tomb in Egypt.

UMBRELLA ■ Umbrellas were invented in China, but the name comes from the Romans, who called them *umbraculum,* meaning "shady place"—so named because at first they were only used to shade people from the sun. Waterproof versions, constructed of oiled paper made from mulberry bark, began appearing in China in the 6th century. The first waterproof umbrellas in England, which began appearing in the 1630s, were made of oiled leather or canvas. Strangely, many people saw the use of such an item as "sinful," declaring that the "godly purpose of rain is to make people wet."

UNCLE SAM ■ There really was an Uncle Sam. His name was Samuel Wilson, and he made his living as a meat inspector during the War of 1812. Uncle Sam, the nickname by which many knew Wilson, was determined to prevent tainted meat from being sent to American troops. To accomplish this, Wilson insisted that all barrels of meat be inspected and stamped with *U.S.* Wilson jokingly claimed that *U.S.* stood for his nickname's initials. Today Uncle Sam is a symbol of our entire federal government.

UNDERDOG ■ The person (or team) most likely to lose a game is called the underdog. The term comes from dog fighting in the Old West. The dog held down, usually by the neck, was certainly the "underdog"—the one most likely to lose.

UTOPIA ■ In 1516, English politician and writer Thomas More wrote a book about a perfect society in which

everyone is completely happy. Originally, More entitled it *Nusquama,* which is Latin for "nowhere." Before publication, he retitled it *Utopia,* Greek for "nowhere." In 1872, English author Samuel Butler kept the tradition alive; he wrote another book about such a place and gave it a name with the same meaning. Entitled *Erehwon,* it is *nowhere* spelled backward.

Of these three words with the same definition, only *utopia* has survived as a term meaning "a perfect world or place."

U2 ■ During the Cold War, the United States and Russia (then called the Soviet Union) had thousands of nuclear weapons aimed at each other, enough to kill everything on Earth. To keep an eye on the Russians, the U.S. military flew spy missions over their country in a secret plane called the U2. Our government thought it was undetectable. It wasn't. In 1960, the Russians shot down one in what has come to be known as the "U2 incident." It almost started World War III. It didn't; instead, it ended up as the name of a politically minded rock group.

Two previous names used by the group were Feedback and The Hype. At one performance, the audience voted on the names *The Hype* and *U2*. The name *U2* won, partly because of the play on words: It sounds like "you too" and "you two."

VANDAL ■ The vandals were a 5th-century Germanic tribe known for their brutality and destructiveness. Among other places, the Vandals conquered Rome, mindlessly smashing and ruining everything in what was then the most beautiful city in the world. The name came to mean anyone who is stupidly and maliciously destructive.

VENEZUELA ■ Venice, a city of canals and rivers, is one of the most beautiful in Italy. When Italian explorers found a beautiful place in South America (with lots of rivers), they named it Little Venice—*Venezuela.*

Vicks® VapoRub® ■ The product was on the market for some time as Richardson's Croup and Pneumonia Cure Salve. Lunsford Richardson, its inventor, was obviously in need of a shorter, catchier name. He changed it to Vicks VapoRub, naming it after his brother-in-law Dr. Joshua Vick.

VOLLEYBALL ■ William Morgan invented the sport in 1895. He originally called it minonette—no one knows why, and no one seems to have the slightest idea what the name means. Around 1900, the name became volleyball—the word *volley* meaning "to hit the ball back and forth over the net."

WALL STREET ■ The name *Wall Street* brings to mind images of high-rise buildings and high finance. But that's not what it was like in the beginning. It got its name in 1654 when New Yorkers built a high wooden wall—a stockade—across the southern tip of Manhattan to protect against attacks by Indians and British soldiers from the north.

By the 17th century, the "wall" was rebuilt as a long row of brick houses. And the path that had once been in front of the stockade became a street—Wall Street.

WASHINGTON, GEORGE ■ The Washington family name has been traced back to 1260 in England. The name at that time was de Wessington. Over the next century, it changed from Wessington to Wassington to Washington.

When he was a kid, George loved listening to the war stories of his half brother Lawrence Washington, who had served with the English in a brief war with Spain.

Ironically, George Washington (1732–1799) was named after King George II of England as a "show of loyalty to the crown"—and then grew up to lead the colonial army in defeating the English in the American Revolution. In the war, he was up against his namesake's son, King George III.

At the age of fourteen, George wanted to join the British Royal Navy. He needed his mother's permission. She wouldn't give it; she said it was "too dangerous."

Welch's® Grape Juice ▪ The Presbyterian church that Dr. Thomas Welch attended in Vineland, New Jersey, forbade the drinking of any alcoholic beverages— including even sacramental wine. In 1896, Dr. Welch, a dentist, successfully pasteurized Concord grape juice to produce an unfermented sacramental wine for fellow parishioners. In 1893, his son, Charles Welch, began marketing Welch's Grape Juice.

Like his father, Charles Welch was a dentist. In a letter to him, Charles's father told him that being a dentist was a more dependable way to make a living. He wrote, "Stick to dentistry, forget about grape juice."

It's kind of scary, and also sad—some people suffer from a rare genetic condition known as werewolf syndrome. Long hair grows all over their bodies and faces, causing them to look very much like werewolves. This disease may have been responsible for some of the legends about werewolves.

WEREWOLVES ▪ In the language of ancient Germany, *were* meant "man." And that is what a werewolf is—a monster that is half man and half wolf.

As late as the 16th century, people accused of being werewolves were executed. One of the most recent of these was a tailor from Paris who, on December 14, 1598, was sentenced to death for being a "half-man, half-beast." A search of his house uncovered a whole barrel full of human bones. The details of his trial—and supposed deeds—were so horrible that when it was over, the judges ordered that all the documents relating to the case be destroyed.

In 19th-century England fictional stories about werewolves were extremely popular. From November 1846 through July 1847, readers in Britain were thrilled by weekly installments (pamphlets costing a penny) of the adventures of Wagner the Wehr-Wolf. Filled with gruesome deeds and endless horrors, such stories were known as bloods or penny dreadfuls.

WHIPPING BOY ■ Today the term refers to someone who is made to take the punishment for another's mistake.

It all began with an outrageous practice during the Middle Ages. If a prince misbehaved, the king or queen would order that he be whipped—knowing full well that he wouldn't be. Instead, a substitute (a commoner) would take the punishment. At all times, at least one whipping boy was kept around the royal household.

WHITE HOUSE ■ In 1759, George Washington married the widowed Martha Custis of Virginia. If he had married someone else, the White House would have a different name.

When George met Martha, she owned a plantation, one that had belonged to her husband. To Martha, the house was a symbol of her childhood and happy times. Her pet name for the place was the White House. George and Martha often stayed there, and George grew to love it as much as his wife did.

George Washington never lived in the White House. John Adams, the second U.S. president, was the first to do so. Even then, it was not yet completed; Mrs. Adams used the East Room to dry laundry.

Almost thirty years later, in 1787, Washington became the first president of the United States. A presidential palace was built of white limestone and whitewashed wood, and Washington called it the White House—not just because it was white, but also in memory of the plantation house he and his wife had loved so much.

Though the name White House was in common use almost from the start, it was merely a nickname until September 1901, when Theodore Roosevelt made it official.

There are 132 rooms in the White House and 35 bathrooms.

Teddy Roosevelt's children used the East Room as a roller-skating rink, and on one occasion, the president staged a boxing match in it.

For recreation, the White House has a tennis court, jogging track, swimming pool, movie theater, billiard room, and bowling lane.

During the War of 1812, the British burned much of the mansion. After it was rebuilt and patched up, it was re-painted white (even much of the original—but smoke-blackened—limestone), further popularizing the name *White House*.

> *What happened to Martha's original "white house"? It was burned to the ground in 1861, the first year of the Civil War. Its last owner was the wife of Robert E. Lee, a descendant of Martha Washington.*

WIFE ■ In early English, the general term for humankind was *mann*. And weaving (then called *wifan*) was the most important skill for a married woman. Thus, a married woman was called a wiff-mann ("weaving person"). Over the centuries, *mann* was out and *wiff* became *wife*.

Wonder Woman™ ■ It's the truth. The creator of Wonder Woman, William Moulton Morrison, a respected psychologist, invented one of the first polygraph machines (lie detectors).

With his Wonder Woman comics (which debuted in December 1941) Morrison expressed his lifelong belief in equal rights for women. In a fictional world dominated by men, Wonder Woman is the world's first and fore-most comic book heroine.

> *William Moulton Morrison wrote under the pan name Charles Moulton.*

Armed with bulletproof bracelets, a magic lasso of truth, and an invisible airplane, she uses intelligence, speed, and strength to thwart evil and promote peace and justice. In "a world torn by the hatreds and wars of men," she is devoted to democracy and "freedom for all womankind." Rather than kill her enemies, she teaches them respect for the rights of others.

In the comic strip, her identity is a secret. She goes by the name of Diana Prince, supposedly a U.S. Army nurse who went to South America to get married.

Morrison's choice of the name *Diana* was no accident. In Roman mythology, Diana is the daughter of the queen of the Amazons and became the powerful goddess of the moon and of hunting.

As both the writer and artist, Morrison fussed and fumed for a long time in coming up with a name for his female equivalent to Superman. After drawing up lists of dozens of names, he decided upon Wonder Woman. Why? Because he liked the way the words sounded together; they alliterated (began with the same letter).

X ▪ Why is an *X* at the end of a letter a symbol of love? In the Middle Ages, people who couldn't read or write signed documents with an *X,* then kissed the *X* as a pledge to abide by the terms of the agreement. In time, the *X* and the kiss became symbolic companions, with the letter *O* eventually added to represent the puckered shape of the mouth when kissing. And because it "goes around," *O* has also come to represent a hug.

Xerox® ▪ One day in 1947, a man named Chester Carlson came knocking at the door of the Haloid Company, a small printing firm. Carlson said he had invented an "electrophotographic apparatus"—a device for making photolike copies of pictures and documents. He expected just to be told to go away, as he already had been by more than twenty other companies. Instead, the people at the Haloid Company realized that Carlson had invented something great; and soon, with Carlson directing production, they were making and selling Haloid Copiers. The name was changed in the early 1950s from Haloid to Xerox. The company's name was short for a word Carlson created to describe the process—xerography, which combines the Greek word for "dry" *(xeros)* with *graphein,* meaning "to write."

XMAS ▪ Sometimes people write *Christmas* as *Xmas.* It looks like nothing more than a casual abbreviation.

It's a great deal more. Early Christians were tortured and killed, especially by the Romans. Just being a Christian was grounds for death. To identify themselves to fellow Christians without attracting attention, they drew or traced the letter *X* in whatever way was handy. The *X* was a sign of the cross and meant "Christ." To write *Christmas* as *Xmas* is not only correct; it recalls a more than two-thousand-year-old custom.

(See Christmas, page 31.)

"YANKEE DOODLE" ■ The song was written by a British army surgeon to make fun of Americans (*Yankee,* at the time, was a derogatory term, and a *doodle* was a fool). Instead of being bothered by it, American soldiers during the American Revolution adopted the song. They sang and played "Yankee Doodle" as a show of patriotism—and in defiance of the British troops.

YANKEES ■ During the 17th century, English and Dutch settlers were fighting for control of large areas of land in what is now the northeastern United States. As so often happens when people are fighting, the settlers from these different countries had some nasty names for one another. No one remembers what the English called the Dutch. But one of the Dutch terms for the English has become an everyday word in our vocabulary—and in the world of sports.

The Dutch called the English Jan Kees. *Jan* is Dutch for "John" and *kees* is Dutch for "cheese." In other words, Dutchmen thought it was funny to refer to an Englishman as John Cheese. (Since people hardly ever bathed then and body odor was usually very strong, the suggestion was that the English looked and smelled pretty "cheesy.")

In time *Jan Kees* became *Yankees.* Today, most Americans are not bothered at all by using this term when referring to themselves. And, of course, one of baseball's most famous teams, the New

For one year (1950) there was a pro football team known as the New York Yanks.

York Yankees, adopted the name in 1913. (For the first ten years of its existence the team was called the New York Highlanders—for the reason that its home field was Hilltop Park, a hastily constructed, all-wood stadium located on one of the highest spots in Manhattan.)

The team actually began in Baltimore. In 1903, the Baltimore franchise folded and was purchased by two New Yorkers for $18,000.

YO-YO ■ Originally a hunting weapon, *yo-yo* comes from Tagalog, the native language of the Philippines, and means "come-come." In France, yo-yos are known as *bandalores;* in England they are called *quizzes.*

> *In San Francisco, in 1979, Dr. Tom Kuhn constructed the largest yo-yo of all time. The monster weighed 256 pounds! To operate it, the yo-yo was suspended from a 150-foot-high crane. The huge yo-yo could be made to go up and down by pulling back and forth on the crane's controls.*

YUCATÁN ■ In 1517, Spanish explorer Francisco Córdoba reached the Yucatán Peninsula in southeast Mexico. When he asked the native people what the region was called, he was told *"Yucatán?"* Not understanding the Spaniard's question, the Indians had responded with a question of their own: *"Yu ca tan?"*—"What are you saying?"

Thinking this was the name of the region, the Spaniards happily sailed home and told everybody they had discovered Yucatán. Today one of the largest states of Mexico, Yucatán is eternalized as "What are you saying?"

Zamboni® ■ How come those big, weird-looking ice-resurfacing vehicles are called Zambonis? Because they were invented in 1942 by teenage brothers Frank and George Zamboni. The brothers built the first one out of an old army Jeep to resurface Iceland, the skating rink in California they'd opened in 1940.

ZIP CODE ■ In 1944, Robert Moon, a Pennsylvania postal director, came up with the idea for address coding in order to speed up the delivery of mail. The five-digit zoning improvement plan codes appeared

> *Until about 1850, letters in the United States were paid for by the persons receiving them, not by the senders.*

> *Until rather recent times, it took weeks—often months—for letters to reach their destination.*

in postal directories in 1963. The name was picked intentionally to have initials forming a word suggesting speed: *ZIP.*

ZOMBIE ■ In Haitian voodoo, a *zombie* is a dead body brought back to life by an evil sorcerer. Zombies are mindless slaves who work endlessly, doing whatever they are told. The word comes from the African term *zumbi,* which means "witch-craft."

Forgotten Words

Anywhen ■ At any time. The term, which originated in southern England, has never known the popularity of its many cousins—*anywhere, anything,* and *anyhow,* for example.

Beblubbered ■ Swollen.

Bellibone ■ In the 16th century, a *bellibone* was an extremely pretty woman. It comes from two French words: *belle* (beautiful) and *bonne* (good).

Bravette ■ Medieval knights in England and France wore bravettes under their armor. These were towel-sized pieces of chain mail that protected their private parts.

Bumblepuppy ■ The original name of tetherball.

Camel-swallower ■ A weak-minded fool who'd believe anything he was told, no matter how ridiculous.

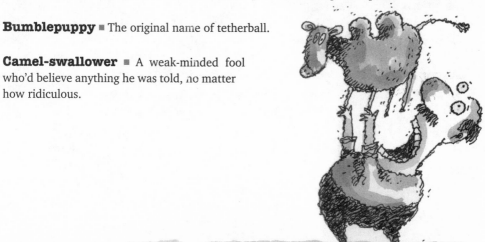

Drizzen ▪ To shrink and dry up.

Emunctories ▪ All the less-than-pleasant sounds and actions occurring during nose blowing.

Farthingale ▪ In Europe in the 16th and 17th centuries, women wore bell-shaped hoop skirts. To make them billow out, they wore an underskirt called a farthingale. The contraption was sort of like a big birdcage of flexible wood or whalebone hanging from the woman's waist—over which the lower part of the dress would go.

Why were they called farthingales? The word is an English rendering of a French word meaning "the young sprig of a tree."

Flepper ▪ The lower lip.

Flesh-spades ▪ During the 18th century, fingernails were called flesh-spades, the idea being that they were like digging tools built right into the flesh of the fingers.

Folberths ▪ The first windshield wipers had to be operated by hand. A passenger (or the driver) would have to turn a crank to make them work. Automatic windshield wipers were invented in 1921. For the first few years of their existence, they were called Folberths, after their inventor and manufacturer. W. M. Folberth.

Geo-graffy ▪ No, this isn't a misspelling of *geography*. It's a beverage that British sailors used to make by boiling a burnt biscuit in water.

Gloppened ▪ Surprised; astonished.

Hoined ▪ Exhausted; overworked.

Idle-worms ▪ As late as the 17th century, little girls were told that "idle worms" would grow between their fingers if they didn't work hard and keep their hands and fingers busy.

Jeopardy-trot ■ Walking at a very fast pace when feeling threatened or in danger.

Keak ■ From the 17th through the 19th centuries, the word meant "to cackle like a witch."

Lip-clap ■ A bygone English word for *kiss*.

Merry-Go-Sorry ■ During the 16th and 17th centuries, a *merry-go-sorry* was a story intended to make someone happy and sad at the same time.

Mubblefubbles ■ In the 19th century, to have the mubblefubbles was to be unhappy for no apparent reason.

Murfles ■ In 15th-century England, *murfles* were freckles. By the 16th century, they had turned into pimples. By the 18th century, almost everybody had forgotten what they were.

Nazzle ■ A little girl who plays tricks or tells lies.

Outcumlins ■ Strangers; people from another neighborhood.

Pig's whisper ■ A whisper that's intentionally loud enough to be heard.

Quakebuttocks ■ Slang term in the Middle Ages for "a coward."

Roxle ■ To make a grunting noise.

Snirtle ■ Giggle. Snicker. During the 18th and 19th centuries, a *snirtler* was someone who laughed behind your back.

Spitel ■ A medieval hospital for lepers and the poor. An observer of a spitel described it in these words: "In one bed . . . lay as many as six persons beside each other, the feet of one to the head of another. In the same bed lay individuals with infectious diseases beside others only slightly unwell; . . . body against body, a woman groaned in the pangs of labor, a typhus patient burned with fever, a consumptive coughed his hollow cough, and a victim of some disease of the skin tore with furious nails his infernally itching integument. . . ."

Turdiform ■ The word meant "like a thrush in shape," the thrush being a bird of the family *Turdae*.

Unky ▪ Lonely.

Vomitory ▪ The door of a large building by which crowds of commoners were let out.

Wurp ▪ In England, from the 10th through the 13th century, a person could wurp at you, or glance. Same thing.

Xanthodont ▪ A person with yellow teeth or a person who looks like a rat or other rodent.

Yaffle ▪ To speak unclearly, as a person without teeth might sound.

Zowerswopped ▪ Foul-tempered; ill-natured.

Bibliography

Oxford Desk Dictionary of People and Places. Edited by Frank Abate. Oxford: Oxford University Press, 1999.

American Heritage Dictionary of the English Language. 4th ed. New York: Houghton Mifflin Company, 2000.

Ammer, Christine. *It's Raining Cats & Dogs— and Other Beastly Expressions.* St. Paul: Paragon House, 1989.

Bartlett, John. *Familiar Quotations.* Boston: Little, Brown and Company, 1980.

Brewer, E. C. *Dictionary of Phrase and Fable.* 8th rev. Revised by John Freeman. New York: Harper & Row, 1964.

Brown, Arch. *Great Cars of the Twentieth Century.* Lincolnwood, IL: Publications International, Ltd., 1991.

Chronicle of the 20th Century. Edited by Daniel Clifton. Mount Kisco, N.Y.: Chronicle Publications, 1987.

Dictionary of American History. 7 vols. Edited by James T. Adams. New York: Charles Scribner's Sons, 1940.

Encyclopedia Britannica. Chicago: Encyclopedia Britannica, Inc., 1970.

Garrison, Webb. *Why You Say It.* New York: Abington Press, 1955.

Larousse Encyclopedia of Mythology. Edited by Robert Graves. New York: Prometheus Press, 1960.

History of Rock & Roll. Edited by J. Miller. New York: Random House, 1980.

Holt, Alfred. *Phrase and Word Origins.* London: Dover Publications, 1961.

Javna, John, and Gordon Javna. *'60s!* New York: St. Martin's Press, 1982.

Kacirk, Jeffrey. *The Word Museum.* New York: Touchstone Books, 2000.

Mencken, H. L. *The American Language.* 3 vols. Abridgement of the 4th edition by Raven I. McDavid, Jr. New York: Alfred A. Knopf, 1963.

Morris, Evan. *The Word Detective.* New York: The Penguin Group, 2000.

Morris, William, and Mary Morris. *Dictionary of Word and Phrase Origins.* New York: Harper & Row, 1962.

New Dictionary of American Slang. Edited by Robert L. Chapman. New York: Harper & Row, 1986.

Rawson, Hugh. *Devious Derivations.* New York: Crown Publishers, 1994.

Rees, Nigel. *Phrases and Sayings.* London: Bloomsbury Publishing, 1995.

Robertson, Patrick. *The Book of Firsts.* New York: Holt, Rinehart and Winston, 1974.

Room, Adrian. *NTC's Dictionary of Trade Name Origins.* Chicago: NTC Publishing Group, 1991.

Severn, Bill. *People Words.* New York: Ives Washburn, Inc. Publishers, 1966.

Wallace, Irving, and David Wallechinsky. *The People's Almanac.* New York: William Morrow & Co., 1987.

Webster's New International Dictionary. 2nd ed. Edited by Alan Neilson. Springfield, MA: G. & C. Merriman Company, 1944.

World Book Encyclopedia. Chicago: World Book–Childcraft International, Inc., 1981.

Index